DATE

LOCATION

GPS

WEATHER CONDITIONS

SPECIES / TYPE

SPECIMEN

TOTAL LENGTH

TYPE OF FOREST

☐ DECIDUOUS		☐ CONIFEROUS
☐ TROPICAL		☐ OTHER

CAP CHARACTERISTICS

CAP COLOR

CAP SHAPE

CAP TEXTURE

CAP DIAMETER

CAP LENGTH

HYMENIUM

SPECIAL PROPERTIES

STALK CHARACTERISTICS

STALK COLOR

STALK SHAPE

STALK TEXTURE

STALK DIAMETER

STALK LENGTH

STALK SURFACE

SPECIAL PROPERTIES

SURROUNDING PLANTS

FAUNA / WILDLIFE

ADDITIONAL NOTE

D1398923

DATE	WEATHER CONDITIONS

DATE

LOCATION

GPS

WEATHER CONDITIONS

🌡 ___   ☀ ⛅ 🌧 ⛈ ❄

🚩 ___   ☐ ☐ ☐ ☐ ☐

SPECIES / TYPE

SPECIMEN #

TOTAL LENGTH

TYPE OF FOREST

☐ DECIDUOUS	☐ CONIFEROUS
☐ TROPICAL	☐ OTHER

CAP CHARACTERISTICS

CAP COLOR

CAP SHAPE

CAP TEXTURE

CAP DIAMETER

CAP LENGTH

HYMENIUM

SPECIAL PROPERTIES

STALK CHARACTERISTICS

STALK COLOR

STALK SHAPE

STALK TEXTURE

STALK DIAMETER

STALK LENGTH

STALK SURFACE

SPECIAL PROPERTIES

SURROUNDING PLANTS

FAUNA / WILDLIFE

ADDITIONAL NOTES

DATE	**WEATHER CONDITIONS**
LOCATION	🌡 —— ☀ ⛅ 🌧 ⛈ ❄
GPS	💨 —— ☐ ☐ ☐ ☐ ☐

SPECIES / TYPE	**TYPE OF FOREST**
SPECIMEN #	☐ DECIDUOUS ☐ CONIFEROUS
TOTAL LENGTH	☐ TROPICAL ☐ OTHER

CAP CHARACTERISTICS

- CAP COLOR
- CAP SHAPE
- CAP TEXTURE
- CAP DIAMETER
- CAP LENGTH
- HYMENIUM
- SPECIAL PROPERTIES

STALK CHARACTERISTICS

- STALK COLOR
- STALK SHAPE
- STALK TEXTURE
- STALK DIAMETER
- STALK LENGTH
- STALK SURFACE
- SPECIAL PROPERTIES

SURROUNDING PLANTS

FAUNA / WILDLIFE

ADDITIONAL NOTES

DATE		WEATHER CONDITIONS

DATE

LOCATION

GPS

WEATHER CONDITIONS

		☀	⛅	🌧	⛈	❄
	—	○	○	○	○	○

SPECIES / TYPE

SPECIMEN #

TOTAL LENGTH

TYPE OF FOREST

○ DECIDUOUS	○ CONIFEROUS
○ TROPICAL	○ OTHER

CAP CHARACTERISTICS

CAP COLOR

CAP SHAPE

CAP TEXTURE

CAP DIAMETER

CAP LENGTH

HYMENIUM

SPECIAL PROPERTIES

STALK CHARACTERISTICS

STALK COLOR

STALK SHAPE

STALK TEXTURE

STALK DIAMETER

STALK LENGTH

STALK SURFACE

SPECIAL PROPERTIES

SURROUNDING PLANTS

FAUNA / WILDLIFE

ADDITIONAL NOTES

DATE

LOCATION

GPS

WEATHER CONDITIONS

SPECIES / TYPE

SPECIMEN

TOTAL LENGTH

TYPE OF FOREST

☐ DECIDUOUS		☐ CONIFEROUS
☐ TROPICAL		☐ OTHER

CAP CHARACTERISTICS

CAP COLOR

CAP SHAPE

CAP TEXTURE

CAP DIAMETER

CAP LENGTH

HYMENIUM

SPECIAL PROPERTIES

STALK CHARACTERISTICS

STALK COLOR

STALK SHAPE

STALK TEXTURE

STALK DIAMETER

STALK LENGTH

STALK SURFACE

SPECIAL PROPERTIES

SURROUNDING PLANTS

FAUNA / WILDLIFE

ADDITIONAL NOTES

DATE	WEATHER CONDITIONS

DATE

LOCATION

GPS

WEATHER CONDITIONS

🌡 ____   ☀ ⛅ 🌧 ⛈ ❄

🚩 ____   ☐ ☐ ☐ ☐ ☐

SPECIES / TYPE

SPECIMEN #

TOTAL LENGTH

TYPE OF FOREST

☐ DECIDUOUS	☐ CONIFEROUS
☐ TROPICAL	☐ OTHER

CAP CHARACTERISTICS

CAP COLOR

CAP SHAPE

CAP TEXTURE

CAP DIAMETER

CAP LENGTH

HYMENIUM

SPECIAL PROPERTIES

STALK CHARACTERISTICS

STALK COLOR

STALK SHAPE

STALK TEXTURE

STALK DIAMETER

STALK LENGTH

STALK SURFACE

SPECIAL PROPERTIES

SURROUNDING PLANTS

FAUNA / WILDLIFE

ADDITIONAL NOTES

DATE

LOCATION

GPS

WEATHER CONDITIONS

[thermometer] ——— ☀ ⛅ 🌧 ⛈ ❄

[anemometer] ——— ☐ ☐ ☐ ☐ ☐

SPECIES / TYPE

SPECIMEN

TOTAL LENGTH

TYPE OF FOREST

| ☐ DECIDUOUS | ☐ CONIFEROUS |
| ☐ TROPICAL | ☐ OTHER |

CAP CHARACTERISTICS

CAP COLOR

CAP SHAPE

CAP TEXTURE

CAP DIAMETER

CAP LENGTH

HYMENIUM

SPECIAL PROPERTIES

STALK CHARACTERISTICS

STALK COLOR

STALK SHAPE

STALK TEXTURE

STALK DIAMETER

STALK LENGTH

STALK SURFACE

SPECIAL PROPERTIES

SURROUNDING PLANTS

FAUNA / WILDLIFE

ADDITIONAL NOTES

📅 DATE		**WEATHER CONDITIONS**					
📍 LOCATION		🌡 ___	☀️	⛅	🌧	⛈	❄️
🧭 GPS		🎏 ___	☐	☐	☐	☐	☐

🔍 SPECIES / TYPE	**TYPE OF FOREST**	
🗂 SPECIMEN #	☐ DECIDUOUS	☐ CONIFEROUS
🍄 TOTAL LENGTH	☐ TROPICAL	☐ OTHER

CAP CHARACTERISTICS	**STALK CHARACTERISTICS**
🍄 CAP COLOR	🍄 STALK COLOR
🍄 CAP SHAPE	🍄 STALK SHAPE
🍄 CAP TEXTURE	🍄 STALK TEXTURE
🍄 CAP DIAMETER	🍄 STALK DIAMETER
🍄 CAP LENGTH	🍄 STALK LENGTH
🍄 HYMENIUM	🍄 STALK SURFACE
🍄 SPECIAL PROPERTIES	🍄 SPECIAL PROPERTIES

SURROUNDING PLANTS	**FAUNA / WILDLIFE**

ADDITIONAL NOTES

DATE

LOCATION

GPS

WEATHER CONDITIONS

SPECIES / TYPE

SPECIMEN

TOTAL LENGTH

TYPE OF FOREST

☐ DECIDUOUS		☐ CONIFEROUS	
☐ TROPICAL		☐ OTHER	

CAP CHARACTERISTICS

CAP COLOR

CAP SHAPE

CAP TEXTURE

CAP DIAMETER

CAP LENGTH

HYMENIUM

SPECIAL PROPERTIES

STALK CHARACTERISTICS

STALK COLOR

STALK SHAPE

STALK TEXTURE

STALK DIAMETER

STALK LENGTH

STALK SURFACE

SPECIAL PROPERTIES

SURROUNDING PLANTS

FAUNA / WILDLIFE

ADDITIONAL NOTES

DATE	WEATHER CONDITIONS

DATE

LOCATION

GPS

WEATHER CONDITIONS

🌡 ———   ☀ ⛅ 🌧 ⛈ ❄

🚩 ———   ☐ ☐ ☐ ☐ ☐

SPECIES / TYPE

SPECIMEN #

TOTAL LENGTH

TYPE OF FOREST

☐ DECIDUOUS	☐ CONIFEROUS
☐ TROPICAL	☐ OTHER

CAP CHARACTERISTICS

CAP COLOR

CAP SHAPE

CAP TEXTURE

CAP DIAMETER

CAP LENGTH

HYMENIUM

SPECIAL PROPERTIES

STALK CHARACTERISTICS

STALK COLOR

STALK SHAPE

STALK TEXTURE

STALK DIAMETER

STALK LENGTH

STALK SURFACE

SPECIAL PROPERTIES

SURROUNDING PLANTS

FAUNA / WILDLIFE

ADDITIONAL NOTES

DATE

LOCATION

GPS

WEATHER CONDITIONS

SPECIES / TYPE

SPECIMEN

TOTAL LENGTH

TYPE OF FOREST

☐ DECIDUOUS	☐ CONIFEROUS
☐ TROPICAL	☐ OTHER

CAP CHARACTERISTICS

CAP COLOR
CAP SHAPE
CAP TEXTURE
CAP DIAMETER
CAP LENGTH
HYMENIUM
SPECIAL PROPERTIES

STALK CHARACTERISTICS

STALK COLOR
STALK SHAPE
STALK TEXTURE
STALK DIAMETER
STALK LENGTH
STALK SURFACE
SPECIAL PROPERTIES

SURROUNDING PLANTS

FAUNA / WILDLIFE

ADDITIONAL NOTES

DATE	WEATHER CONDITIONS

DATE

LOCATION

GPS

WEATHER CONDITIONS

SPECIES / TYPE

SPECIMEN #

TOTAL LENGTH

TYPE OF FOREST

☐ DECIDUOUS   ☐ CONIFEROUS

☐ TROPICAL   ☐ OTHER

CAP CHARACTERISTICS

CAP COLOR

CAP SHAPE

CAP TEXTURE

CAP DIAMETER

CAP LENGTH

HYMENIUM

SPECIAL PROPERTIES

STALK CHARACTERISTICS

STALK COLOR

STALK SHAPE

STALK TEXTURE

STALK DIAMETER

STALK LENGTH

STALK SURFACE

SPECIAL PROPERTIES

SURROUNDING PLANTS

FAUNA / WILDLIFE

ADDITIONAL NOTES

DATE

LOCATION

GPS

WEATHER CONDITIONS

		☀	⛅	🌧	⛈	❄
🌡	___					
🚩	___	☐	☐	☐	☐	☐

SPECIES / TYPE

SPECIMEN

TOTAL LENGTH

TYPE OF FOREST

☐ DECIDUOUS	☐ CONIFEROUS
☐ TROPICAL	☐ OTHER

CAP CHARACTERISTICS

CAP COLOR

CAP SHAPE

CAP TEXTURE

CAP DIAMETER

CAP LENGTH

HYMENIUM

SPECIAL PROPERTIES

STALK CHARACTERISTICS

STALK COLOR

STALK SHAPE

STALK TEXTURE

STALK DIAMETER

STALK LENGTH

STALK SURFACE

SPECIAL PROPERTIES

SURROUNDING PLANTS

FAUNA / WILDLIFE

ADDITIONAL NOTES

DATE

LOCATION

GPS

WEATHER CONDITIONS

	☀	⛅	🌧	⛈	❄
	☐	☐	☐	☐	☐

SPECIES / TYPE

SPECIMEN

TOTAL LENGTH

TYPE OF FOREST

☐ DECIDUOUS	☐ CONIFEROUS
☐ TROPICAL	☐ OTHER

CAP CHARACTERISTICS

CAP COLOR

CAP SHAPE

CAP TEXTURE

CAP DIAMETER

CAP LENGTH

HYMENIUM

SPECIAL PROPERTIES

STALK CHARACTERISTICS

STALK COLOR

STALK SHAPE

STALK TEXTURE

STALK DIAMETER

STALK LENGTH

STALK SURFACE

SPECIAL PROPERTIES

SURROUNDING PLANTS

FAUNA / WILDLIFE

ADDITIONAL NOTES

DATE

LOCATION

GPS

WEATHER CONDITIONS

🌡 —   ☀ ⛅ 🌧 ⛈ ❄

🚩 —   ☐ ☐ ☐ ☐ ☐

SPECIES / TYPE

SPECIMEN

TOTAL LENGTH

TYPE OF FOREST

| ☐ DECIDUOUS | ☐ CONIFEROUS |
| ☐ TROPICAL | ☐ OTHER |

CAP CHARACTERISTICS

CAP COLOR

CAP SHAPE

CAP TEXTURE

CAP DIAMETER

CAP LENGTH

HYMENIUM

SPECIAL PROPERTIES

STALK CHARACTERISTICS

STALK COLOR

STALK SHAPE

STALK TEXTURE

STALK DIAMETER

STALK LENGTH

STALK SURFACE

SPECIAL PROPERTIES

SURROUNDING PLANTS

FAUNA / WILDLIFE

ADDITIONAL NOTES

DATE	WEATHER CONDITIONS

DATE

LOCATION

GPS

WEATHER CONDITIONS

☼ ⛅ 🌧 ⛈ ❄

☐ ☐ ☐ ☐ ☐

SPECIES / TYPE

SPECIMEN #

TOTAL LENGTH

TYPE OF FOREST

☐ DECIDUOUS   ☐ CONIFEROUS

☐ TROPICAL   ☐ OTHER

CAP CHARACTERISTICS

CAP COLOR

CAP SHAPE

CAP TEXTURE

CAP DIAMETER

CAP LENGTH

HYMENIUM

SPECIAL PROPERTIES

STALK CHARACTERISTICS

STALK COLOR

STALK SHAPE

STALK TEXTURE

STALK DIAMETER

STALK LENGTH

STALK SURFACE

SPECIAL PROPERTIES

SURROUNDING PLANTS

FAUNA / WILDLIFE

ADDITIONAL NOTES

DATE

LOCATION

GPS

WEATHER CONDITIONS

SPECIES / TYPE

SPECIMEN

TOTAL LENGTH

TYPE OF FOREST

☐ DECIDUOUS		☐ CONIFEROUS	
☐ TROPICAL		☐ OTHER	

CAP CHARACTERISTICS

CAP COLOR

CAP SHAPE

CAP TEXTURE

CAP DIAMETER

CAP LENGTH

HYMENIUM

SPECIAL PROPERTIES

STALK CHARACTERISTICS

STALK COLOR

STALK SHAPE

STALK TEXTURE

STALK DIAMETER

STALK LENGTH

STALK SURFACE

SPECIAL PROPERTIES

SURROUNDING PLANTS

FAUNA / WILDLIFE

ADDITIONAL NOTES

DATE
LOCATION
GPS

WEATHER CONDITIONS

🌡 —— ☀ ⛅ 🌧 ⛈ ❄

🏳 —— ☐ ☐ ☐ ☐ ☐

SPECIES / TYPE
SPECIMEN #
TOTAL LENGTH

TYPE OF FOREST

☐ DECIDUOUS	☐ CONIFEROUS
☐ TROPICAL	☐ OTHER

CAP CHARACTERISTICS

CAP COLOR
CAP SHAPE
CAP TEXTURE
CAP DIAMETER
CAP LENGTH
HYMENIUM
SPECIAL PROPERTIES

STALK CHARACTERISTICS

STALK COLOR
STALK SHAPE
STALK TEXTURE
STALK DIAMETER
STALK LENGTH
STALK SURFACE
SPECIAL PROPERTIES

SURROUNDING PLANTS

FAUNA / WILDLIFE

ADDITIONAL NOTES

DATE

LOCATION

GPS

WEATHER CONDITIONS

SPECIES / TYPE

SPECIMEN

TOTAL LENGTH

TYPE OF FOREST

☐ DECIDUOUS	☐ CONIFEROUS
☐ TROPICAL	☐ OTHER

CAP CHARACTERISTICS

CAP COLOR

CAP SHAPE

CAP TEXTURE

CAP DIAMETER

CAP LENGTH

HYMENIUM

SPECIAL PROPERTIES

STALK CHARACTERISTICS

STALK COLOR

STALK SHAPE

STALK TEXTURE

STALK DIAMETER

STALK LENGTH

STALK SURFACE

SPECIAL PROPERTIES

SURROUNDING PLANTS

FAUNA / WILDLIFE

ADDITIONAL NOTES

| 📅 **DATE** |
| 📍 **LOCATION** |
| 🧭 **GPS** |

WEATHER CONDITIONS

🌡 ____ ☀ ⛅ ☁ 🌧 ❄

🚩 ____ ☐ ☐ ☐ ☐ ☐

| 🔍 **SPECIES / TYPE** |
| 📇 **SPECIMEN #** |
| 🍄 **TOTAL LENGTH** |

TYPE OF FOREST

| ☐ DECIDUOUS | ☐ CONIFEROUS |
| ☐ TROPICAL | ☐ OTHER |

CAP CHARACTERISTICS

| 🍄 CAP COLOR |
| 🍄 CAP SHAPE |
| CAP TEXTURE |
| CAP DIAMETER |
| 🍄 CAP LENGTH |
| HYMENIUM |
| 🍄 SPECIAL PROPERTIES |

STALK CHARACTERISTICS

| 🍄 STALK COLOR |
| 🍄 STALK SHAPE |
| STALK TEXTURE |
| STALK DIAMETER |
| 🍄 STALK LENGTH |
| 🍄 STALK SURFACE |
| 🍄 SPECIAL PROPERTIES |

SURROUNDING PLANTS

FAUNA / WILDLIFE

ADDITIONAL NOTES

DATE

LOCATION

GPS

WEATHER CONDITIONS

SPECIES / TYPE

SPECIMEN

TOTAL LENGTH

TYPE OF FOREST

☐ DECIDUOUS		☐ CONIFEROUS	
☐ TROPICAL		☐ OTHER	

CAP CHARACTERISTICS

CAP COLOR

CAP SHAPE

CAP TEXTURE

CAP DIAMETER

CAP LENGTH

HYMENIUM

SPECIAL PROPERTIES

STALK CHARACTERISTICS

STALK COLOR

STALK SHAPE

STALK TEXTURE

STALK DIAMETER

STALK LENGTH

STALK SURFACE

SPECIAL PROPERTIES

SURROUNDING PLANTS

FAUNA / WILDLIFE

ADDITIONAL NOTES

DATE	**WEATHER CONDITIONS**

DATE		WEATHER CONDITIONS
LOCATION		☀ ⛅ 🌧 ⛈ ❄
GPS		☐ ☐ ☐ ☐ ☐

SPECIES / TYPE		TYPE OF FOREST	
SPECIMEN #		☐ DECIDUOUS	☐ CONIFEROUS
TOTAL LENGTH		☐ TROPICAL	☐ OTHER

CAP CHARACTERISTICS	STALK CHARACTERISTICS
CAP COLOR	STALK COLOR
CAP SHAPE	STALK SHAPE
CAP TEXTURE	STALK TEXTURE
CAP DIAMETER	STALK DIAMETER
CAP LENGTH	STALK LENGTH
HYMENIUM	STALK SURFACE
SPECIAL PROPERTIES	SPECIAL PROPERTIES

SURROUNDING PLANTS	FAUNA / WILDLIFE

ADDITIONAL NOTES

DATE

LOCATION

GPS

WEATHER CONDITIONS

SPECIES / TYPE

SPECIMEN

TOTAL LENGTH

TYPE OF FOREST

☐ DECIDUOUS	☐ CONIFEROUS
☐ TROPICAL	☐ OTHER

CAP CHARACTERISTICS

CAP COLOR

CAP SHAPE

CAP TEXTURE

CAP DIAMETER

CAP LENGTH

HYMENIUM

SPECIAL PROPERTIES

STALK CHARACTERISTICS

STALK COLOR

STALK SHAPE

STALK TEXTURE

STALK DIAMETER

STALK LENGTH

STALK SURFACE

SPECIAL PROPERTIES

SURROUNDING PLANTS

FAUNA / WILDLIFE

ADDITIONAL NOTES

DATE

LOCATION

GPS

WEATHER CONDITIONS

SPECIES / TYPE

SPECIMEN

TOTAL LENGTH

TYPE OF FOREST

☐ DECIDUOUS		☐ CONIFEROUS	
☐ TROPICAL		☐ OTHER	

CAP CHARACTERISTICS

CAP COLOR

CAP SHAPE

CAP TEXTURE

CAP DIAMETER

CAP LENGTH

HYMENIUM

SPECIAL PROPERTIES

STALK CHARACTERISTICS

STALK COLOR

STALK SHAPE

STALK TEXTURE

STALK DIAMETER

STALK LENGTH

STALK SURFACE

SPECIAL PROPERTIES

SURROUNDING PLANTS

FAUNA / WILDLIFE

ADDITIONAL NOTES

DATE	WEATHER CONDITIONS

DATE
LOCATION
GPS

WEATHER CONDITIONS

SPECIES / TYPE	TYPE OF FOREST

SPECIES / TYPE
SPECIMEN #
TOTAL LENGTH

TYPE OF FOREST

DECIDUOUS	CONIFEROUS
TROPICAL	OTHER

CAP CHARACTERISTICS

CAP COLOR
CAP SHAPE
CAP TEXTURE
CAP DIAMETER
CAP LENGTH
HYMENIUM
SPECIAL PROPERTIES

STALK CHARACTERISTICS

STALK COLOR
STALK SHAPE
STALK TEXTURE
STALK DIAMETER
STALK LENGTH
STALK SURFACE
SPECIAL PROPERTIES

SURROUNDING PLANTS

FAUNA / WILDLIFE

ADDITIONAL NOTES

DATE	
LOCATION	
GPS	

WEATHER CONDITIONS

🌡 ____   ☀ ⛅ 🌧 ⛈ ❄

🏳 ____   ☐ ☐ ☐ ☐ ☐

SPECIES / TYPE	
SPECIMEN #	
TOTAL LENGTH	

TYPE OF FOREST

☐ DECIDUOUS	☐ CONIFEROUS
☐ TROPICAL	☐ OTHER

CAP CHARACTERISTICS

CAP COLOR
CAP SHAPE
CAP TEXTURE
CAP DIAMETER
CAP LENGTH
HYMENIUM
SPECIAL PROPERTIES

STALK CHARACTERISTICS

STALK COLOR
STALK SHAPE
STALK TEXTURE
STALK DIAMETER
STALK LENGTH
STALK SURFACE
SPECIAL PROPERTIES

SURROUNDING PLANTS

FAUNA / WILDLIFE

ADDITIONAL NOTES

DATE

LOCATION

GPS

WEATHER CONDITIONS

🌡 ___ ☀ ⛅ 🌧 ⛈ ❄
🚩 ___ ☐ ☐ ☐ ☐ ☐

SPECIES / TYPE

SPECIMEN

TOTAL LENGTH

TYPE OF FOREST

| ☐ DECIDUOUS | ☐ CONIFEROUS |
| ☐ TROPICAL | ☐ OTHER |

CAP CHARACTERISTICS

| CAP COLOR |
| CAP SHAPE |
| CAP TEXTURE |
| CAP DIAMETER |
| CAP LENGTH |
| HYMENIUM |
| SPECIAL PROPERTIES |

STALK CHARACTERISTICS

| STALK COLOR |
| STALK SHAPE |
| STALK TEXTURE |
| STALK DIAMETER |
| STALK LENGTH |
| STALK SURFACE |
| SPECIAL PROPERTIES |

SURROUNDING PLANTS

FAUNA / WILDLIFE

ADDITIONAL NOTES

DATE	WEATHER CONDITIONS

DATE

LOCATION

GPS

WEATHER CONDITIONS

☐ ☐ ☐ ☐ ☐

SPECIES / TYPE

SPECIMEN #

TOTAL LENGTH

TYPE OF FOREST

☐ DECIDUOUS	☐ CONIFEROUS
☐ TROPICAL	☐ OTHER

CAP CHARACTERISTICS

CAP COLOR

CAP SHAPE

CAP TEXTURE

CAP DIAMETER

CAP LENGTH

HYMENIUM

SPECIAL PROPERTIES

STALK CHARACTERISTICS

STALK COLOR

STALK SHAPE

STALK TEXTURE

STALK DIAMETER

STALK LENGTH

STALK SURFACE

SPECIAL PROPERTIES

SURROUNDING PLANTS

FAUNA / WILDLIFE

ADDITIONAL NOTES

DATE	WEATHER CONDITIONS

DATE

LOCATION

GPS

WEATHER CONDITIONS

🌡 —   ☀ ⛅ ☁ 🌧 ❄

🚩 —   ☐ ☐ ☐ ☐ ☐

SPECIES / TYPE

SPECIMEN #

TOTAL LENGTH

TYPE OF FOREST

☐ DECIDUOUS   ☐ CONIFEROUS

☐ TROPICAL   ☐ OTHER

CAP CHARACTERISTICS

CAP COLOR

CAP SHAPE

CAP TEXTURE

CAP DIAMETER

CAP LENGTH

HYMENIUM

SPECIAL PROPERTIES

STALK CHARACTERISTICS

STALK COLOR

STALK SHAPE

STALK TEXTURE

STALK DIAMETER

STALK LENGTH

STALK SURFACE

SPECIAL PROPERTIES

SURROUNDING PLANTS

FAUNA / WILDLIFE

ADDITIONAL NOTES

DATE	
LOCATION	
GPS	

WEATHER CONDITIONS

☀ ⛅ 🌧 ⛈ ❄

☐ ☐ ☐ ☐ ☐

SPECIES / TYPE	
SPECIMEN #	
TOTAL LENGTH	

TYPE OF FOREST

☐ DECIDUOUS	☐ CONIFEROUS
☐ TROPICAL	☐ OTHER

CAP CHARACTERISTICS

CAP COLOR
CAP SHAPE
CAP TEXTURE
CAP DIAMETER
CAP LENGTH
HYMENIUM
SPECIAL PROPERTIES

STALK CHARACTERISTICS

STALK COLOR
STALK SHAPE
STALK TEXTURE
STALK DIAMETER
STALK LENGTH
STALK SURFACE
SPECIAL PROPERTIES

SURROUNDING PLANTS

FAUNA / WILDLIFE

ADDITIONAL NOTES

DATE

LOCATION

GPS

WEATHER CONDITIONS

SPECIES / TYPE

SPECIMEN

TOTAL LENGTH

TYPE OF FOREST

☐ DECIDUOUS	☐ CONIFEROUS
☐ TROPICAL	☐ OTHER

CAP CHARACTERISTICS

CAP COLOR
CAP SHAPE
CAP TEXTURE
CAP DIAMETER
CAP LENGTH
HYMENIUM
SPECIAL PROPERTIES

STALK CHARACTERISTICS

STALK COLOR
STALK SHAPE
STALK TEXTURE
STALK DIAMETER
STALK LENGTH
STALK SURFACE
SPECIAL PROPERTIES

SURROUNDING PLANTS

FAUNA / WILDLIFE

ADDITIONAL NOTES

DATE

LOCATION

GPS

WEATHER CONDITIONS

☐ ☐ ☐ ☐ ☐

SPECIES / TYPE

SPECIMEN

TOTAL LENGTH

TYPE OF FOREST

| ☐ DECIDUOUS | ☐ CONIFEROUS |
| ☐ TROPICAL | ☐ OTHER |

CAP CHARACTERISTICS

CAP COLOR

CAP SHAPE

CAP TEXTURE

CAP DIAMETER

CAP LENGTH

HYMENIUM

SPECIAL PROPERTIES

STALK CHARACTERISTICS

STALK COLOR

STALK SHAPE

STALK TEXTURE

STALK DIAMETER

STALK LENGTH

STALK SURFACE

SPECIAL PROPERTIES

SURROUNDING PLANTS

FAUNA / WILDLIFE

ADDITIONAL NOTES

DATE

LOCATION

GPS

WEATHER CONDITIONS

(thermometer) —— ☀ ⛅ 🌧 ⛈ ❄

(wind) —— ☐ ☐ ☐ ☐ ☐

SPECIES / TYPE

SPECIMEN

TOTAL LENGTH

TYPE OF FOREST

| ☐ DECIDUOUS | ☐ CONIFEROUS |
| ☐ TROPICAL | ☐ OTHER |

CAP CHARACTERISTICS

CAP COLOR

CAP SHAPE

CAP TEXTURE

CAP DIAMETER

CAP LENGTH

HYMENIUM

SPECIAL PROPERTIES

STALK CHARACTERISTICS

STALK COLOR

STALK SHAPE

STALK TEXTURE

STALK DIAMETER

STALK LENGTH

STALK SURFACE

SPECIAL PROPERTIES

SURROUNDING PLANTS

FAUNA / WILDLIFE

ADDITIONAL NOTES

DATE	WEATHER CONDITIONS

DATE

LOCATION

GPS

WEATHER CONDITIONS

🌡 ___ ☀ ⛅ 🌧 ⛈ ❄

🚩 ___ ☐ ☐ ☐ ☐ ☐

SPECIES / TYPE

SPECIMEN #

TOTAL LENGTH

TYPE OF FOREST

☐ DECIDUOUS	☐ CONIFEROUS
☐ TROPICAL	☐ OTHER

CAP CHARACTERISTICS

CAP COLOR

CAP SHAPE

CAP TEXTURE

CAP DIAMETER

CAP LENGTH

HYMENIUM

SPECIAL PROPERTIES

STALK CHARACTERISTICS

STALK COLOR

STALK SHAPE

STALK TEXTURE

STALK DIAMETER

STALK LENGTH

STALK SURFACE

SPECIAL PROPERTIES

SURROUNDING PLANTS

FAUNA / WILDLIFE

ADDITIONAL NOTES

DATE

LOCATION

GPS

WEATHER CONDITIONS

SPECIES / TYPE

SPECIMEN

TOTAL LENGTH

TYPE OF FOREST

☐ DECIDUOUS	☐ CONIFEROUS
☐ TROPICAL	☐ OTHER

CAP CHARACTERISTICS

CAP COLOR

CAP SHAPE

CAP TEXTURE

CAP DIAMETER

CAP LENGTH

HYMENIUM

SPECIAL PROPERTIES

STALK CHARACTERISTICS

STALK COLOR

STALK SHAPE

STALK TEXTURE

STALK DIAMETER

STALK LENGTH

STALK SURFACE

SPECIAL PROPERTIES

SURROUNDING PLANTS

FAUNA / WILDLIFE

ADDITIONAL NOTES

DATE

LOCATION

GPS

WEATHER CONDITIONS

SPECIES / TYPE

SPECIMEN

TOTAL LENGTH

TYPE OF FOREST

| ☐ DECIDUOUS | ☐ CONIFEROUS |
| ☐ TROPICAL | ☐ OTHER |

CAP CHARACTERISTICS

CAP COLOR

CAP SHAPE

CAP TEXTURE

CAP DIAMETER

CAP LENGTH

HYMENIUM

SPECIAL PROPERTIES

STALK CHARACTERISTICS

STALK COLOR

STALK SHAPE

STALK TEXTURE

STALK DIAMETER

STALK LENGTH

STALK SURFACE

SPECIAL PROPERTIES

SURROUNDING PLANTS

FAUNA / WILDLIFE

ADDITIONAL NOTES

DATE

LOCATION

GPS

WEATHER CONDITIONS

		☀	⛅	☁	🌧	❄
🌡	___					
🚩	___	☐	☐	☐	☐	☐

SPECIES / TYPE

SPECIMEN

TOTAL LENGTH

TYPE OF FOREST

☐ DECIDUOUS	☐ CONIFEROUS
☐ TROPICAL	☐ OTHER

CAP CHARACTERISTICS

CAP COLOR

CAP SHAPE

CAP TEXTURE

CAP DIAMETER

CAP LENGTH

HYMENIUM

SPECIAL PROPERTIES

STALK CHARACTERISTICS

STALK COLOR

STALK SHAPE

STALK TEXTURE

STALK DIAMETER

STALK LENGTH

STALK SURFACE

SPECIAL PROPERTIES

SURROUNDING PLANTS

FAUNA / WILDLIFE

ADDITIONAL NOTES

DATE	WEATHER CONDITIONS

DATE

LOCATION

GPS

WEATHER CONDITIONS

☀ ⛅ 🌧 ⛈ ❄

☐ ☐ ☐ ☐ ☐

SPECIES / TYPE

SPECIMEN #

TOTAL LENGTH

TYPE OF FOREST

☐ DECIDUOUS	☐ CONIFEROUS
☐ TROPICAL	☐ OTHER

CAP CHARACTERISTICS

CAP COLOR

CAP SHAPE

CAP TEXTURE

CAP DIAMETER

CAP LENGTH

HYMENIUM

SPECIAL PROPERTIES

STALK CHARACTERISTICS

STALK COLOR

STALK SHAPE

STALK TEXTURE

STALK DIAMETER

STALK LENGTH

STALK SURFACE

SPECIAL PROPERTIES

SURROUNDING PLANTS

FAUNA / WILDLIFE

ADDITIONAL NOTES

DATE	**WEATHER CONDITIONS**

DATE
LOCATION
GPS

WEATHER CONDITIONS

SPECIES / TYPE
SPECIMEN
TOTAL LENGTH

TYPE OF FOREST

☐ DECIDUOUS	☐ CONIFEROUS
☐ TROPICAL	☐ OTHER

CAP CHARACTERISTICS

- CAP COLOR
- CAP SHAPE
- CAP TEXTURE
- CAP DIAMETER
- CAP LENGTH
- HYMENIUM
- SPECIAL PROPERTIES

STALK CHARACTERISTICS

- STALK COLOR
- STALK SHAPE
- STALK TEXTURE
- STALK DIAMETER
- STALK LENGTH
- STALK SURFACE
- SPECIAL PROPERTIES

SURROUNDING PLANTS

FAUNA / WILDLIFE

ADDITIONAL NOTES

DATE	WEATHER CONDITIONS

DATE

LOCATION

GPS

WEATHER CONDITIONS

🌡️ _____ ☀️ ⛅ 🌧️ ⛈️ ❄️

🚩 _____ ☐ ☐ ☐ ☐ ☐

SPECIES / TYPE

SPECIMEN #

TOTAL LENGTH

TYPE OF FOREST

☐ DECIDUOUS	☐ CONIFEROUS
☐ TROPICAL	☐ OTHER

CAP CHARACTERISTICS

CAP COLOR

CAP SHAPE

CAP TEXTURE

CAP DIAMETER

CAP LENGTH

HYMENIUM

SPECIAL PROPERTIES

STALK CHARACTERISTICS

STALK COLOR

STALK SHAPE

STALK TEXTURE

STALK DIAMETER

STALK LENGTH

STALK SURFACE

SPECIAL PROPERTIES

SURROUNDING PLANTS

FAUNA / WILDLIFE

ADDITIONAL NOTES

DATE		WEATHER CONDITIONS					
LOCATION			☀	⛅	☁	⛈	❄
GPS			☐	☐	☐	☐	☐

SPECIES / TYPE		TYPE OF FOREST	
SPECIMEN #		☐ DECIDUOUS	☐ CONIFEROUS
TOTAL LENGTH		☐ TROPICAL	☐ OTHER

CAP CHARACTERISTICS	STALK CHARACTERISTICS
CAP COLOR	STALK COLOR
CAP SHAPE	STALK SHAPE
CAP TEXTURE	STALK TEXTURE
CAP DIAMETER	STALK DIAMETER
CAP LENGTH	STALK LENGTH
HYMENIUM	STALK SURFACE
SPECIAL PROPERTIES	SPECIAL PROPERTIES

SURROUNDING PLANTS	FAUNA / WILDLIFE

ADDITIONAL NOTES

DATE

LOCATION

GPS

WEATHER CONDITIONS

☐ ☐ ☐ ☐ ☐

SPECIES / TYPE

SPECIMEN

TOTAL LENGTH

TYPE OF FOREST

☐ DECIDUOUS		☐ CONIFEROUS
☐ TROPICAL		☐ OTHER

CAP CHARACTERISTICS

- CAP COLOR
- CAP SHAPE
- CAP TEXTURE
- CAP DIAMETER
- CAP LENGTH
- HYMENIUM
- SPECIAL PROPERTIES

STALK CHARACTERISTICS

- STALK COLOR
- STALK SHAPE
- STALK TEXTURE
- STALK DIAMETER
- STALK LENGTH
- STALK SURFACE
- SPECIAL PROPERTIES

SURROUNDING PLANTS

FAUNA / WILDLIFE

ADDITIONAL NOTES

DATE	
LOCATION	
GPS	

WEATHER CONDITIONS

🌡️ ____   ☀️ ⛅ 🌧️ ⛈️ ❄️

🎐 ____   ☐ ☐ ☐ ☐ ☐

SPECIES / TYPE	
SPECIMEN #	
TOTAL LENGTH	

TYPE OF FOREST

☐ DECIDUOUS	☐ CONIFEROUS
☐ TROPICAL	☐ OTHER

CAP CHARACTERISTICS

CAP COLOR	
CAP SHAPE	
CAP TEXTURE	
CAP DIAMETER	
CAP LENGTH	
HYMENIUM	
SPECIAL PROPERTIES	

STALK CHARACTERISTICS

STALK COLOR	
STALK SHAPE	
STALK TEXTURE	
STALK DIAMETER	
STALK LENGTH	
STALK SURFACE	
SPECIAL PROPERTIES	

SURROUNDING PLANTS

FAUNA / WILDLIFE

ADDITIONAL NOTES

DATE

LOCATION

GPS

WEATHER CONDITIONS

🌡 —— ☀ ⛅ 🌧 ⛈ ❄

🚩 —— ☐ ☐ ☐ ☐ ☐

SPECIES / TYPE

SPECIMEN

TOTAL LENGTH

TYPE OF FOREST

☐ DECIDUOUS	☐ CONIFEROUS
☐ TROPICAL	☐ OTHER

CAP CHARACTERISTICS

CAP COLOR

CAP SHAPE

CAP TEXTURE

CAP DIAMETER

CAP LENGTH

HYMENIUM

SPECIAL PROPERTIES

STALK CHARACTERISTICS

STALK COLOR

STALK SHAPE

STALK TEXTURE

STALK DIAMETER

STALK LENGTH

STALK SURFACE

SPECIAL PROPERTIES

SURROUNDING PLANTS

FAUNA / WILDLIFE

ADDITIONAL NOTES

DATE

LOCATION

GPS

WEATHER CONDITIONS

🌡 ____ ☀ ⛅ 🌧 ⛈ ❄

🚩 ____ ☐ ☐ ☐ ☐ ☐

SPECIES / TYPE

SPECIMEN

TOTAL LENGTH

TYPE OF FOREST

| ☐ DECIDUOUS | ☐ CONIFEROUS |
| ☐ TROPICAL | ☐ OTHER |

CAP CHARACTERISTICS

CAP COLOR

CAP SHAPE

CAP TEXTURE

CAP DIAMETER

CAP LENGTH

HYMENIUM

SPECIAL PROPERTIES

STALK CHARACTERISTICS

STALK COLOR

STALK SHAPE

STALK TEXTURE

STALK DIAMETER

STALK LENGTH

STALK SURFACE

SPECIAL PROPERTIES

SURROUNDING PLANTS

FAUNA / WILDLIFE

ADDITIONAL NOTES

DATE

LOCATION

GPS

WEATHER CONDITIONS

SPECIES / TYPE

SPECIMEN

TOTAL LENGTH

TYPE OF FOREST

☐ DECIDUOUS		☐ CONIFEROUS	
☐ TROPICAL		☐ OTHER	

CAP CHARACTERISTICS

CAP COLOR

CAP SHAPE

CAP TEXTURE

CAP DIAMETER

CAP LENGTH

HYMENIUM

SPECIAL PROPERTIES

STALK CHARACTERISTICS

STALK COLOR

STALK SHAPE

STALK TEXTURE

STALK DIAMETER

STALK LENGTH

STALK SURFACE

SPECIAL PROPERTIES

SURROUNDING PLANTS

FAUNA / WILDLIFE

ADDITIONAL NOTES

DATE	WEATHER CONDITIONS

WEATHER CONDITIONS

🌡 —— ☀ ⛅ 🌧 ⛈ ❄

🚩 —— ☐ ☐ ☐ ☐ ☐

DATE
LOCATION
GPS

SPECIES / TYPE

SPECIES / TYPE
SPECIMEN #
TOTAL LENGTH

TYPE OF FOREST

☐ DECIDUOUS	☐ CONIFEROUS
☐ TROPICAL	☐ OTHER

CAP CHARACTERISTICS

- CAP COLOR
- CAP SHAPE
- CAP TEXTURE
- CAP DIAMETER
- CAP LENGTH
- HYMENIUM
- SPECIAL PROPERTIES

STALK CHARACTERISTICS

- STALK COLOR
- STALK SHAPE
- STALK TEXTURE
- STALK DIAMETER
- STALK LENGTH
- STALK SURFACE
- SPECIAL PROPERTIES

SURROUNDING PLANTS

FAUNA / WILDLIFE

ADDITIONAL NOTES

DATE

LOCATION

GPS

WEATHER CONDITIONS

SPECIES / TYPE

SPECIMEN

TOTAL LENGTH

TYPE OF FOREST

| ☐ DECIDUOUS | ☐ CONIFEROUS |
| ☐ TROPICAL | ☐ OTHER |

CAP CHARACTERISTICS

CAP COLOR

CAP SHAPE

CAP TEXTURE

CAP DIAMETER

CAP LENGTH

HYMENIUM

SPECIAL PROPERTIES

STALK CHARACTERISTICS

STALK COLOR

STALK SHAPE

STALK TEXTURE

STALK DIAMETER

STALK LENGTH

STALK SURFACE

SPECIAL PROPERTIES

SURROUNDING PLANTS

FAUNA / WILDLIFE

ADDITIONAL NOTES

DATE

LOCATION

GPS

WEATHER CONDITIONS

☀ ⛅ 🌧 ⛈ ❄

☐ ☐ ☐ ☐ ☐

SPECIES / TYPE

SPECIMEN

TOTAL LENGTH

TYPE OF FOREST

☐ DECIDUOUS	☐ CONIFEROUS
☐ TROPICAL	☐ OTHER

CAP CHARACTERISTICS

CAP COLOR

CAP SHAPE

CAP TEXTURE

CAP DIAMETER

CAP LENGTH

HYMENIUM

SPECIAL PROPERTIES

STALK CHARACTERISTICS

STALK COLOR

STALK SHAPE

STALK TEXTURE

STALK DIAMETER

STALK LENGTH

STALK SURFACE

SPECIAL PROPERTIES

SURROUNDING PLANTS

FAUNA / WILDLIFE

ADDITIONAL NOTES

DATE		WEATHER CONDITIONS

DATE

LOCATION

GPS

WEATHER CONDITIONS

🌡 ____ ☀ ⛅ 🌧 ⛈ ❄

🌡 ____ ☐ ☐ ☐ ☐ ☐

SPECIES / TYPE

SPECIMEN #

TOTAL LENGTH

TYPE OF FOREST

☐ DECIDUOUS	☐ CONIFEROUS
☐ TROPICAL	☐ OTHER

CAP CHARACTERISTICS

CAP COLOR

CAP SHAPE

CAP TEXTURE

CAP DIAMETER

CAP LENGTH

HYMENIUM

SPECIAL PROPERTIES

STALK CHARACTERISTICS

STALK COLOR

STALK SHAPE

STALK TEXTURE

STALK DIAMETER

STALK LENGTH

STALK SURFACE

SPECIAL PROPERTIES

SURROUNDING PLANTS

FAUNA / WILDLIFE

ADDITIONAL NOTES

DATE	**WEATHER CONDITIONS**

DATE
LOCATION
GPS

WEATHER CONDITIONS

☀ ⛅ 🌧 ⛈ ❄

☐ ☐ ☐ ☐ ☐

SPECIES / TYPE
SPECIMEN #
TOTAL LENGTH

TYPE OF FOREST

☐ DECIDUOUS	☐ CONIFEROUS
☐ TROPICAL	☐ OTHER

CAP CHARACTERISTICS

CAP COLOR
CAP SHAPE
CAP TEXTURE
CAP DIAMETER
CAP LENGTH
HYMENIUM
SPECIAL PROPERTIES

STALK CHARACTERISTICS

STALK COLOR
STALK SHAPE
STALK TEXTURE
STALK DIAMETER
STALK LENGTH
STALK SURFACE
SPECIAL PROPERTIES

SURROUNDING PLANTS

FAUNA / WILDLIFE

ADDITIONAL NOTES

DATE	**WEATHER CONDITIONS**
LOCATION	
GPS	

DATE

LOCATION

GPS

WEATHER CONDITIONS

SPECIES / TYPE	**TYPE OF FOREST**
SPECIMEN #	☐ DECIDUOUS ☐ CONIFEROUS
TOTAL LENGTH	☐ TROPICAL ☐ OTHER

CAP CHARACTERISTICS

CAP COLOR

CAP SHAPE

CAP TEXTURE

CAP DIAMETER

CAP LENGTH

HYMENIUM

SPECIAL PROPERTIES

STALK CHARACTERISTICS

STALK COLOR

STALK SHAPE

STALK TEXTURE

STALK DIAMETER

STALK LENGTH

STALK SURFACE

SPECIAL PROPERTIES

SURROUNDING PLANTS

FAUNA / WILDLIFE

ADDITIONAL NOTES

DATE	
LOCATION	
GPS	

WEATHER CONDITIONS

		☀	⛅	🌧	⛈	❄
🌡	—					
🚩	—	☐	☐	☐	☐	☐

SPECIES / TYPE	
SPECIMEN #	
TOTAL LENGTH	

TYPE OF FOREST

☐ DECIDUOUS	☐ CONIFEROUS
☐ TROPICAL	☐ OTHER

CAP CHARACTERISTICS

CAP COLOR
CAP SHAPE
CAP TEXTURE
CAP DIAMETER
CAP LENGTH
HYMENIUM
SPECIAL PROPERTIES

STALK CHARACTERISTICS

STALK COLOR
STALK SHAPE
STALK TEXTURE
STALK DIAMETER
STALK LENGTH
STALK SURFACE
SPECIAL PROPERTIES

SURROUNDING PLANTS

FAUNA / WILDLIFE

ADDITIONAL NOTES

DATE

LOCATION

GPS

WEATHER CONDITIONS

SPECIES / TYPE

SPECIMEN

TOTAL LENGTH

TYPE OF FOREST

☐ DECIDUOUS	☐ CONIFEROUS
☐ TROPICAL	☐ OTHER

CAP CHARACTERISTICS

CAP COLOR
CAP SHAPE
CAP TEXTURE
CAP DIAMETER
CAP LENGTH
HYMENIUM
SPECIAL PROPERTIES

STALK CHARACTERISTICS

STALK COLOR
STALK SHAPE
STALK TEXTURE
STALK DIAMETER
STALK LENGTH
STALK SURFACE
SPECIAL PROPERTIES

SURROUNDING PLANTS

FAUNA / WILDLIFE

ADDITIONAL NOTES

DATE	WEATHER CONDITIONS

DATE

LOCATION

GPS

WEATHER CONDITIONS

☀ ⛅ 🌧 ⛈ ❄

☐ ☐ ☐ ☐ ☐

SPECIES / TYPE

SPECIMEN #

TOTAL LENGTH

TYPE OF FOREST

☐ DECIDUOUS	☐ CONIFEROUS
☐ TROPICAL	☐ OTHER

CAP CHARACTERISTICS

CAP COLOR

CAP SHAPE

CAP TEXTURE

CAP DIAMETER

CAP LENGTH

HYMENIUM

SPECIAL PROPERTIES

STALK CHARACTERISTICS

STALK COLOR

STALK SHAPE

STALK TEXTURE

STALK DIAMETER

STALK LENGTH

STALK SURFACE

SPECIAL PROPERTIES

SURROUNDING PLANTS

FAUNA / WILDLIFE

ADDITIONAL NOTES

| DATE | WEATHER CONDITIONS |

DATE
LOCATION
GPS

WEATHER CONDITIONS

SPECIES / TYPE
SPECIMEN
TOTAL LENGTH

TYPE OF FOREST

☐ DECIDUOUS	☐ CONIFEROUS
☐ TROPICAL	☐ OTHER

CAP CHARACTERISTICS

| CAP COLOR |
| CAP SHAPE |
| CAP TEXTURE |
| CAP DIAMETER |
| CAP LENGTH |
| HYMENIUM |
| SPECIAL PROPERTIES |

STALK CHARACTERISTICS

| STALK COLOR |
| STALK SHAPE |
| STALK TEXTURE |
| STALK DIAMETER |
| STALK LENGTH |
| STALK SURFACE |
| SPECIAL PROPERTIES |

SURROUNDING PLANTS

FAUNA / WILDLIFE

ADDITIONAL NOTES

DATE

LOCATION

GPS

WEATHER CONDITIONS

🌡 —— ☀️ ⛅ 🌧 ⛈ ❄️

🚩 —— ☐   ☐   ☐   ☐   ☐

SPECIES / TYPE

SPECIMEN

TOTAL LENGTH

TYPE OF FOREST

☐ DECIDUOUS	☐ CONIFEROUS
☐ TROPICAL	☐ OTHER

CAP CHARACTERISTICS

CAP COLOR

CAP SHAPE

CAP TEXTURE

CAP DIAMETER

CAP LENGTH

HYMENIUM

SPECIAL PROPERTIES

STALK CHARACTERISTICS

STALK COLOR

STALK SHAPE

STALK TEXTURE

STALK DIAMETER

STALK LENGTH

STALK SURFACE

SPECIAL PROPERTIES

SURROUNDING PLANTS

FAUNA / WILDLIFE

ADDITIONAL NOTES

DATE		WEATHER CONDITIONS

DATE

LOCATION

GPS

WEATHER CONDITIONS

SPECIES / TYPE

SPECIMEN

TOTAL LENGTH

TYPE OF FOREST

☐ DECIDUOUS	☐ CONIFEROUS
☐ TROPICAL	☐ OTHER

CAP CHARACTERISTICS

CAP COLOR

CAP SHAPE

CAP TEXTURE

CAP DIAMETER

CAP LENGTH

HYMENIUM

SPECIAL PROPERTIES

STALK CHARACTERISTICS

STALK COLOR

STALK SHAPE

STALK TEXTURE

STALK DIAMETER

STALK LENGTH

STALK SURFACE

SPECIAL PROPERTIES

SURROUNDING PLANTS

FAUNA / WILDLIFE

ADDITIONAL NOTES

DATE

LOCATION

GPS

WEATHER CONDITIONS

Temperature: ———

Wind: ———

☀ ☐   ⛅ ☐   🌧 ☐   ⛈ ☐   ❄ ☐

SPECIES / TYPE

SPECIMEN

TOTAL LENGTH

TYPE OF FOREST

☐ DECIDUOUS	☐ CONIFEROUS
☐ TROPICAL	☐ OTHER

CAP CHARACTERISTICS

CAP COLOR

CAP SHAPE

CAP TEXTURE

CAP DIAMETER

CAP LENGTH

HYMENIUM

SPECIAL PROPERTIES

STALK CHARACTERISTICS

STALK COLOR

STALK SHAPE

STALK TEXTURE

STALK DIAMETER

STALK LENGTH

STALK SURFACE

SPECIAL PROPERTIES

SURROUNDING PLANTS

FAUNA / WILDLIFE

ADDITIONAL NOTES

DATE	WEATHER CONDITIONS

DATE

LOCATION

GPS

WEATHER CONDITIONS

🌡 _____ ☀ 🌤 🌧 ⛈ ❄

🎏 _____ ☐ ☐ ☐ ☐ ☐

SPECIES / TYPE

SPECIMEN #

TOTAL LENGTH

TYPE OF FOREST

☐ DECIDUOUS ☐ CONIFEROUS

☐ TROPICAL ☐ OTHER

CAP CHARACTERISTICS

CAP COLOR

CAP SHAPE

CAP TEXTURE

CAP DIAMETER

CAP LENGTH

HYMENIUM

SPECIAL PROPERTIES

STALK CHARACTERISTICS

STALK COLOR

STALK SHAPE

STALK TEXTURE

STALK DIAMETER

STALK LENGTH

STALK SURFACE

SPECIAL PROPERTIES

SURROUNDING PLANTS

FAUNA / WILDLIFE

ADDITIONAL NOTES

DATE

LOCATION

GPS

WEATHER CONDITIONS

☐ ☐ ☐ ☐ ☐

SPECIES / TYPE

SPECIMEN

TOTAL LENGTH

TYPE OF FOREST

☐ DECIDUOUS	☐ CONIFEROUS
☐ TROPICAL	☐ OTHER

CAP CHARACTERISTICS

CAP COLOR

CAP SHAPE

CAP TEXTURE

CAP DIAMETER

CAP LENGTH

HYMENIUM

SPECIAL PROPERTIES

STALK CHARACTERISTICS

STALK COLOR

STALK SHAPE

STALK TEXTURE

STALK DIAMETER

STALK LENGTH

STALK SURFACE

SPECIAL PROPERTIES

SURROUNDING PLANTS

FAUNA / WILDLIFE

ADDITIONAL NOTES

DATE	WEATHER CONDITIONS

LOCATION	☀ ⛅ 🌧 ⛈ ❄

GPS	☐ ☐ ☐ ☐ ☐

SPECIES / TYPE	TYPE OF FOREST

SPECIMEN #	☐ DECIDUOUS	☐ CONIFEROUS
TOTAL LENGTH	☐ TROPICAL	☐ OTHER

CAP CHARACTERISTICS

CAP COLOR
CAP SHAPE
CAP TEXTURE
CAP DIAMETER
CAP LENGTH
HYMENIUM
SPECIAL PROPERTIES

STALK CHARACTERISTICS

STALK COLOR
STALK SHAPE
STALK TEXTURE
STALK DIAMETER
STALK LENGTH
STALK SURFACE
SPECIAL PROPERTIES

SURROUNDING PLANTS

FAUNA / WILDLIFE

ADDITIONAL NOTES

DATE	
LOCATION	
GPS	

WEATHER CONDITIONS

🌡 ____ ☀ ⛅ 🌧 ⛈ ❄

🚩 ____ ☐ ☐ ☐ ☐ ☐

SPECIES / TYPE	
SPECIMEN #	
TOTAL LENGTH	

TYPE OF FOREST

☐ DECIDUOUS	☐ CONIFEROUS
☐ TROPICAL	☐ OTHER

CAP CHARACTERISTICS

CAP COLOR	
CAP SHAPE	
CAP TEXTURE	
CAP DIAMETER	
CAP LENGTH	
HYMENIUM	
SPECIAL PROPERTIES	

STALK CHARACTERISTICS

STALK COLOR	
STALK SHAPE	
STALK TEXTURE	
STALK DIAMETER	
STALK LENGTH	
STALK SURFACE	
SPECIAL PROPERTIES	

SURROUNDING PLANTS

FAUNA / WILDLIFE

ADDITIONAL NOTES

DATE	
LOCATION	
GPS	

WEATHER CONDITIONS

🌡 —— ☀ ⛅ 🌧 ⛈ ❄

🎐 —— ☐ ☐ ☐ ☐ ☐

SPECIES / TYPE	
SPECIMEN #	
TOTAL LENGTH	

TYPE OF FOREST

☐ DECIDUOUS	☐ CONIFEROUS
☐ TROPICAL	☐ OTHER

CAP CHARACTERISTICS

CAP COLOR	
CAP SHAPE	
CAP TEXTURE	
CAP DIAMETER	
CAP LENGTH	
HYMENIUM	
SPECIAL PROPERTIES	

STALK CHARACTERISTICS

STALK COLOR	
STALK SHAPE	
STALK TEXTURE	
STALK DIAMETER	
STALK LENGTH	
STALK SURFACE	
SPECIAL PROPERTIES	

SURROUNDING PLANTS

FAUNA / WILDLIFE

ADDITIONAL NOTES

DATE

LOCATION

GPS

WEATHER CONDITIONS

🌡 _____ ☀ ⛅ 🌧 ⛈ ❄

🚩 _____ ☐ ☐ ☐ ☐ ☐

SPECIES / TYPE

SPECIMEN

TOTAL LENGTH

TYPE OF FOREST

☐ DECIDUOUS		☐ CONIFEROUS
☐ TROPICAL		☐ OTHER

CAP CHARACTERISTICS

CAP COLOR

CAP SHAPE

CAP TEXTURE

CAP DIAMETER

CAP LENGTH

HYMENIUM

SPECIAL PROPERTIES

STALK CHARACTERISTICS

STALK COLOR

STALK SHAPE

STALK TEXTURE

STALK DIAMETER

STALK LENGTH

STALK SURFACE

SPECIAL PROPERTIES

SURROUNDING PLANTS

FAUNA / WILDLIFE

ADDITIONAL NOTES

DATE

LOCATION

GPS

WEATHER CONDITIONS

SPECIES / TYPE

SPECIMEN

TOTAL LENGTH

TYPE OF FOREST

☐ DECIDUOUS		☐ CONIFEROUS
☐ TROPICAL		☐ OTHER

CAP CHARACTERISTICS

CAP COLOR

CAP SHAPE

CAP TEXTURE

CAP DIAMETER

CAP LENGTH

HYMENIUM

SPECIAL PROPERTIES

STALK CHARACTERISTICS

STALK COLOR

STALK SHAPE

STALK TEXTURE

STALK DIAMETER

STALK LENGTH

STALK SURFACE

SPECIAL PROPERTIES

SURROUNDING PLANTS

FAUNA / WILDLIFE

ADDITIONAL NOTES

| DATE | WEATHER CONDITIONS |

DATE

LOCATION

GPS

WEATHER CONDITIONS

☼ ⛅ 🌧 ⛈ ❄

☐ ☐ ☐ ☐ ☐

SPECIES / TYPE

SPECIMEN #

TOTAL LENGTH

TYPE OF FOREST

☐ DECIDUOUS ☐ CONIFEROUS

☐ TROPICAL ☐ OTHER

CAP CHARACTERISTICS

CAP COLOR

CAP SHAPE

CAP TEXTURE

CAP DIAMETER

CAP LENGTH

HYMENIUM

SPECIAL PROPERTIES

STALK CHARACTERISTICS

STALK COLOR

STALK SHAPE

STALK TEXTURE

STALK DIAMETER

STALK LENGTH

STALK SURFACE

SPECIAL PROPERTIES

SURROUNDING PLANTS

FAUNA / WILDLIFE

ADDITIONAL NOTES

📅 DATE		**WEATHER CONDITIONS**
📍 LOCATION		🌡️ —— ☀️ ⛅ 🌧️ ⛈️ ❄️
🧭 GPS		🚩 —— ☐ ☐ ☐ ☐ ☐

🔍 SPECIES / TYPE	**TYPE OF FOREST**	
🗄️ SPECIMEN #	☐ DECIDUOUS	☐ CONIFEROUS
🍄 TOTAL LENGTH	☐ TROPICAL	☐ OTHER

CAP CHARACTERISTICS	**STALK CHARACTERISTICS**
🍄 CAP COLOR	🍄 STALK COLOR
🍄 CAP SHAPE	🍄 STALK SHAPE
⚬ CAP TEXTURE	⚬ STALK TEXTURE
CAP DIAMETER	STALK DIAMETER
🍄 CAP LENGTH	🍄 STALK LENGTH
◎ HYMENIUM	🍄 STALK SURFACE
🍄 SPECIAL PROPERTIES	🍄 SPECIAL PROPERTIES

SURROUNDING PLANTS	**FAUNA / WILDLIFE**

ADDITIONAL NOTES

DATE

LOCATION

GPS

WEATHER CONDITIONS

🌡 —— ☀ ⛅ 🌧 ⛈ ❄

🚩 —— ☐ ☐ ☐ ☐ ☐

SPECIES / TYPE

SPECIMEN

TOTAL LENGTH

TYPE OF FOREST

☐ DECIDUOUS	☐ CONIFEROUS
☐ TROPICAL	☐ OTHER

CAP CHARACTERISTICS

CAP COLOR

CAP SHAPE

CAP TEXTURE

CAP DIAMETER

CAP LENGTH

HYMENIUM

SPECIAL PROPERTIES

STALK CHARACTERISTICS

STALK COLOR

STALK SHAPE

STALK TEXTURE

STALK DIAMETER

STALK LENGTH

STALK SURFACE

SPECIAL PROPERTIES

SURROUNDING PLANTS

FAUNA / WILDLIFE

ADDITIONAL NOTES

DATE

LOCATION

GPS

SPECIES / TYPE

SPECIMEN

TOTAL LENGTH

TYPE OF FOREST

DECIDUOUS	CONIFEROUS
TROPICAL	OTHER

CAP CHARACTERISTICS

CAP COLOR
CAP SHAPE
CAP TEXTURE
CAP DIAMETER
CAP LENGTH
HYMENIUM
SPECIAL PROPERTIES

STALK CHARACTERISTICS

STALK COLOR
STALK SHAPE
STALK TEXTURE
STALK DIAMETER
STALK LENGTH
STALK SURFACE
SPECIAL PROPERTIES

SURROUNDING PLANTS

FAUNA / WILDLIFE

ADDITIONAL NOTES

DATE	WEATHER CONDITIONS

DATE	
LOCATION	
GPS	

WEATHER CONDITIONS

🌡 ____ ☀ ⛅ 🌧 ⛈ ❄

🚩 ____ ☐ ☐ ☐ ☐ ☐

SPECIES / TYPE	
SPECIMEN #	
TOTAL LENGTH	

TYPE OF FOREST

☐ DECIDUOUS	☐ CONIFEROUS
☐ TROPICAL	☐ OTHER

CAP CHARACTERISTICS

CAP COLOR	
CAP SHAPE	
CAP TEXTURE	
CAP DIAMETER	
CAP LENGTH	
HYMENIUM	
SPECIAL PROPERTIES	

STALK CHARACTERISTICS

STALK COLOR	
STALK SHAPE	
STALK TEXTURE	
STALK DIAMETER	
STALK LENGTH	
STALK SURFACE	
SPECIAL PROPERTIES	

SURROUNDING PLANTS

FAUNA / WILDLIFE

ADDITIONAL NOTES

DATE	WEATHER CONDITIONS

DATE

LOCATION

GPS

WEATHER CONDITIONS

🌡 —— ☀ ⛅ 🌧 ⛈ ❄

🎏 —— ☐ ☐ ☐ ☐ ☐

SPECIES / TYPE

SPECIMEN #

TOTAL LENGTH

TYPE OF FOREST

☐ DECIDUOUS	☐ CONIFEROUS
☐ TROPICAL	☐ OTHER

CAP CHARACTERISTICS

CAP COLOR

CAP SHAPE

CAP TEXTURE

CAP DIAMETER

CAP LENGTH

HYMENIUM

SPECIAL PROPERTIES

STALK CHARACTERISTICS

STALK COLOR

STALK SHAPE

STALK TEXTURE

STALK DIAMETER

STALK LENGTH

STALK SURFACE

SPECIAL PROPERTIES

SURROUNDING PLANTS

FAUNA / WILDLIFE

ADDITIONAL NOTES

DATE

LOCATION

GPS

WEATHER CONDITIONS

Temperature: ——   ☀ ⛅ 🌧 ⛈ ❄

Wind: ——   ☐ ☐ ☐ ☐ ☐

SPECIES / TYPE

SPECIMEN

TOTAL LENGTH

TYPE OF FOREST

☐ DECIDUOUS	☐ CONIFEROUS
☐ TROPICAL	☐ OTHER

CAP CHARACTERISTICS

CAP COLOR

CAP SHAPE

CAP TEXTURE

CAP DIAMETER

CAP LENGTH

HYMENIUM

SPECIAL PROPERTIES

STALK CHARACTERISTICS

STALK COLOR

STALK SHAPE

STALK TEXTURE

STALK DIAMETER

STALK LENGTH

STALK SURFACE

SPECIAL PROPERTIES

SURROUNDING PLANTS

FAUNA / WILDLIFE

ADDITIONAL NOTES

DATE

LOCATION

GPS

WEATHER CONDITIONS

Temperature: ___

Wind: ___

☀ ⛅ 🌧 ⛈ ❄

☐ ☐ ☐ ☐ ☐

SPECIES / TYPE

SPECIMEN

TOTAL LENGTH

TYPE OF FOREST

☐	DECIDUOUS	☐	CONIFEROUS
☐	TROPICAL	☐	OTHER

CAP CHARACTERISTICS

- CAP COLOR
- CAP SHAPE
- CAP TEXTURE
- CAP DIAMETER
- CAP LENGTH
- HYMENIUM
- SPECIAL PROPERTIES

STALK CHARACTERISTICS

- STALK COLOR
- STALK SHAPE
- STALK TEXTURE
- STALK DIAMETER
- STALK LENGTH
- STALK SURFACE
- SPECIAL PROPERTIES

SURROUNDING PLANTS

FAUNA / WILDLIFE

ADDITIONAL NOTES

📅 **DATE**	
📍 **LOCATION**	
🧭 **GPS**	

WEATHER CONDITIONS

🌡️ ____	☀️	⛅	☁️	⛈️	❄️
🚩 ____	☐	☐	☐	☐	☐

🔍 **SPECIES / TYPE**	
📇 **SPECIMEN #**	
📏 **TOTAL LENGTH**	

TYPE OF FOREST

☐ DECIDUOUS	☐ CONIFEROUS
☐ TROPICAL	☐ OTHER

CAP CHARACTERISTICS

CAP COLOR	
CAP SHAPE	
CAP TEXTURE	
CAP DIAMETER	
CAP LENGTH	
HYMENIUM	
SPECIAL PROPERTIES	

STALK CHARACTERISTICS

STALK COLOR	
STALK SHAPE	
STALK TEXTURE	
STALK DIAMETER	
STALK LENGTH	
STALK SURFACE	
SPECIAL PROPERTIES	

SURROUNDING PLANTS

FAUNA / WILDLIFE

ADDITIONAL NOTES

DATE	WEATHER CONDITIONS

DATE

LOCATION

GPS

WEATHER CONDITIONS

		☼	⛅	☁	⛈	❄
🌡	—	☐	☐	☐	☐	☐
🚩	—					

SPECIES / TYPE

SPECIMEN #

TOTAL LENGTH

TYPE OF FOREST

☐ DECIDUOUS	☐ CONIFEROUS
☐ TROPICAL	☐ OTHER

CAP CHARACTERISTICS

CAP COLOR

CAP SHAPE

CAP TEXTURE

CAP DIAMETER

CAP LENGTH

HYMENIUM

SPECIAL PROPERTIES

STALK CHARACTERISTICS

STALK COLOR

STALK SHAPE

STALK TEXTURE

STALK DIAMETER

STALK LENGTH

STALK SURFACE

SPECIAL PROPERTIES

SURROUNDING PLANTS

FAUNA / WILDLIFE

ADDITIONAL NOTES

DATE

LOCATION

GPS

WEATHER CONDITIONS

SPECIES / TYPE

SPECIMEN

TOTAL LENGTH

TYPE OF FOREST

☐ DECIDUOUS	☐ CONIFEROUS
☐ TROPICAL	☐ OTHER

CAP CHARACTERISTICS

CAP COLOR

CAP SHAPE

CAP TEXTURE

CAP DIAMETER

CAP LENGTH

HYMENIUM

SPECIAL PROPERTIES

STALK CHARACTERISTICS

STALK COLOR

STALK SHAPE

STALK TEXTURE

STALK DIAMETER

STALK LENGTH

STALK SURFACE

SPECIAL PROPERTIES

SURROUNDING PLANTS

FAUNA / WILDLIFE

ADDITIONAL NOTES

DATE

LOCATION

GPS

WEATHER CONDITIONS

SPECIES / TYPE

SPECIMEN

TOTAL LENGTH

TYPE OF FOREST

| ☐ DECIDUOUS | ☐ CONIFEROUS |
| ☐ TROPICAL | ☐ OTHER |

CAP CHARACTERISTICS

CAP COLOR

CAP SHAPE

CAP TEXTURE

CAP DIAMETER

CAP LENGTH

HYMENIUM

SPECIAL PROPERTIES

STALK CHARACTERISTICS

STALK COLOR

STALK SHAPE

STALK TEXTURE

STALK DIAMETER

STALK LENGTH

STALK SURFACE

SPECIAL PROPERTIES

SURROUNDING PLANTS

FAUNA / WILDLIFE

ADDITIONAL NOTES

DATE

LOCATION

GPS

WEATHER CONDITIONS

🌡 ___   ☀ ⛅ 🌧 ⛈ ❄

🏳 ___   ☐ ☐ ☐ ☐ ☐

SPECIES / TYPE

SPECIMEN

TOTAL LENGTH

TYPE OF FOREST

| ☐ DECIDUOUS | ☐ CONIFEROUS |
| ☐ TROPICAL | ☐ OTHER |

CAP CHARACTERISTICS

CAP COLOR

CAP SHAPE

CAP TEXTURE

CAP DIAMETER

CAP LENGTH

HYMENIUM

SPECIAL PROPERTIES

STALK CHARACTERISTICS

STALK COLOR

STALK SHAPE

STALK TEXTURE

STALK DIAMETER

STALK LENGTH

STALK SURFACE

SPECIAL PROPERTIES

SURROUNDING PLANTS

FAUNA / WILDLIFE

ADDITIONAL NOTES

DATE	**WEATHER CONDITIONS**

DATE	
LOCATION	
GPS	

Weather Conditions:
Temperature: ___ ☀ ⛅ ☁ 🌧 ⛈ ❄
Wind: ___ ☐ ☐ ☐ ☐ ☐

SPECIES / TYPE	**TYPE OF FOREST**

SPECIES / TYPE	
SPECIMEN #	
TOTAL LENGTH	

TYPE OF FOREST	
☐ DECIDUOUS	☐ CONIFEROUS
☐ TROPICAL	☐ OTHER

CAP CHARACTERISTICS	**STALK CHARACTERISTICS**

CAP CHARACTERISTICS
CAP COLOR
CAP SHAPE
CAP TEXTURE
CAP DIAMETER
CAP LENGTH
HYMENIUM
SPECIAL PROPERTIES

STALK CHARACTERISTICS
STALK COLOR
STALK SHAPE
STALK TEXTURE
STALK DIAMETER
STALK LENGTH
STALK SURFACE
SPECIAL PROPERTIES

SURROUNDING PLANTS	**FAUNA / WILDLIFE**

SURROUNDING PLANTS

FAUNA / WILDLIFE

ADDITIONAL NOTES

DATE

LOCATION

GPS

WEATHER CONDITIONS

SPECIES / TYPE

SPECIMEN

TOTAL LENGTH

TYPE OF FOREST

☐ DECIDUOUS		☐ CONIFEROUS
☐ TROPICAL		☐ OTHER

CAP CHARACTERISTICS

CAP COLOR

CAP SHAPE

CAP TEXTURE

CAP DIAMETER

CAP LENGTH

HYMENIUM

SPECIAL PROPERTIES

STALK CHARACTERISTICS

STALK COLOR

STALK SHAPE

STALK TEXTURE

STALK DIAMETER

STALK LENGTH

STALK SURFACE

SPECIAL PROPERTIES

SURROUNDING PLANTS

FAUNA / WILDLIFE

ADDITIONAL NOTES

DATE	**WEATHER CONDITIONS**

LOCATION

GPS

| 🌡 ___ | ☀ | ⛅ | 🌧 | ⛈ | ❄ |
| 🌬 ___ | ☐ | ☐ | ☐ | ☐ | ☐ |

SPECIES / TYPE

SPECIMEN #

TOTAL LENGTH

TYPE OF FOREST

☐ DECIDUOUS	☐ CONIFEROUS
☐ TROPICAL	☐ OTHER

CAP CHARACTERISTICS

CAP COLOR

CAP SHAPE

CAP TEXTURE

CAP DIAMETER

CAP LENGTH

HYMENIUM

SPECIAL PROPERTIES

STALK CHARACTERISTICS

STALK COLOR

STALK SHAPE

STALK TEXTURE

STALK DIAMETER

STALK LENGTH

STALK SURFACE

SPECIAL PROPERTIES

SURROUNDING PLANTS

FAUNA / WILDLIFE

ADDITIONAL NOTES

📅 **DATE**	
📍 **LOCATION**	
🧭 **GPS**	

WEATHER CONDITIONS

🌡 —— ☀️ ⛅ 🌧 ⛈ ❄️

🚩 —— ☐ ☐ ☐ ☐ ☐

🔍 **SPECIES / TYPE**	
🗓 **SPECIMEN #**	
🍄 **TOTAL LENGTH**	

TYPE OF FOREST

☐ DECIDUOUS	☐ CONIFEROUS
☐ TROPICAL	☐ OTHER

CAP CHARACTERISTICS

🍄 CAP COLOR	
🍄 CAP SHAPE	
🔶 CAP TEXTURE	
⭕ CAP DIAMETER	
🍄 CAP LENGTH	
◎ HYMENIUM	
🍄 SPECIAL PROPERTIES	

STALK CHARACTERISTICS

🍄 STALK COLOR	
🍄 STALK SHAPE	
🔶 STALK TEXTURE	
⭕ STALK DIAMETER	
🍄 STALK LENGTH	
🍄 STALK SURFACE	
🍄 SPECIAL PROPERTIES	

SURROUNDING PLANTS

FAUNA / WILDLIFE

ADDITIONAL NOTES

DATE	
LOCATION	
GPS	

WEATHER CONDITIONS

🌡 ___ ☀ ⛅ 🌧 ⛈ ❄

🎏 ___ ☐ ☐ ☐ ☐ ☐

SPECIES / TYPE	
SPECIMEN #	
TOTAL LENGTH	

TYPE OF FOREST

☐ DECIDUOUS	☐ CONIFEROUS
☐ TROPICAL	☐ OTHER

CAP CHARACTERISTICS

CAP COLOR	
CAP SHAPE	
CAP TEXTURE	
CAP DIAMETER	
CAP LENGTH	
HYMENIUM	
SPECIAL PROPERTIES	

STALK CHARACTERISTICS

STALK COLOR	
STALK SHAPE	
STALK TEXTURE	
STALK DIAMETER	
STALK LENGTH	
STALK SURFACE	
SPECIAL PROPERTIES	

SURROUNDING PLANTS

FAUNA / WILDLIFE

ADDITIONAL NOTES

DATE

LOCATION

GPS

WEATHER CONDITIONS

☐ ☐ ☐ ☐ ☐

SPECIES / TYPE

SPECIMEN

TOTAL LENGTH

TYPE OF FOREST

| ☐ DECIDUOUS | ☐ CONIFEROUS |
| ☐ TROPICAL | ☐ OTHER |

CAP CHARACTERISTICS

CAP COLOR

CAP SHAPE

CAP TEXTURE

CAP DIAMETER

CAP LENGTH

HYMENIUM

SPECIAL PROPERTIES

STALK CHARACTERISTICS

STALK COLOR

STALK SHAPE

STALK TEXTURE

STALK DIAMETER

STALK LENGTH

STALK SURFACE

SPECIAL PROPERTIES

SURROUNDING PLANTS

FAUNA / WILDLIFE

ADDITIONAL NOTES

DATE
LOCATION
GPS

WEATHER CONDITIONS

🌡 —— ☀ ⛅ 🌧 ⛈ ❄

🚩 —— ☐ ☐ ☐ ☐ ☐

SPECIES / TYPE
SPECIMEN #
TOTAL LENGTH

TYPE OF FOREST

☐ DECIDUOUS	☐ CONIFEROUS
☐ TROPICAL	☐ OTHER

CAP CHARACTERISTICS

CAP COLOR
CAP SHAPE
CAP TEXTURE
CAP DIAMETER
CAP LENGTH
HYMENIUM
SPECIAL PROPERTIES

STALK CHARACTERISTICS

STALK COLOR
STALK SHAPE
STALK TEXTURE
STALK DIAMETER
STALK LENGTH
STALK SURFACE
SPECIAL PROPERTIES

SURROUNDING PLANTS

FAUNA / WILDLIFE

ADDITIONAL NOTES

DATE	WEATHER CONDITIONS

DATE

LOCATION

GPS

WEATHER CONDITIONS

🌡 _____ ☀ ⛅ 🌧 ⛈ ❄

🚩 _____ ☐ ☐ ☐ ☐ ☐

SPECIES / TYPE

SPECIMEN #

TOTAL LENGTH

TYPE OF FOREST

☐ DECIDUOUS ☐ CONIFEROUS

☐ TROPICAL ☐ OTHER

CAP CHARACTERISTICS

CAP COLOR

CAP SHAPE

CAP TEXTURE

CAP DIAMETER

CAP LENGTH

HYMENIUM

SPECIAL PROPERTIES

STALK CHARACTERISTICS

STALK COLOR

STALK SHAPE

STALK TEXTURE

STALK DIAMETER

STALK LENGTH

STALK SURFACE

SPECIAL PROPERTIES

SURROUNDING PLANTS

FAUNA / WILDLIFE

ADDITIONAL NOTES

DATE	**WEATHER CONDITIONS**

DATE
LOCATION
GPS

WEATHER CONDITIONS

🌡 —— ☀ ⛅ 🌧 ⛈ ❄
🚩 —— ☐ ☐ ☐ ☐ ☐

SPECIES / TYPE
SPECIMEN #
TOTAL LENGTH

TYPE OF FOREST

☐ DECIDUOUS	☐ CONIFEROUS
☐ TROPICAL	☐ OTHER

CAP CHARACTERISTICS

CAP COLOR
CAP SHAPE
CAP TEXTURE
CAP DIAMETER
CAP LENGTH
HYMENIUM
SPECIAL PROPERTIES

STALK CHARACTERISTICS

STALK COLOR
STALK SHAPE
STALK TEXTURE
STALK DIAMETER
STALK LENGTH
STALK SURFACE
SPECIAL PROPERTIES

SURROUNDING PLANTS

FAUNA / WILDLIFE

ADDITIONAL NOTES

DATE

LOCATION

GPS

WEATHER CONDITIONS

SPECIES / TYPE

SPECIMEN

TOTAL LENGTH

TYPE OF FOREST

| ☐ DECIDUOUS | ☐ CONIFEROUS |
| ☐ TROPICAL | ☐ OTHER |

CAP CHARACTERISTICS

CAP COLOR

CAP SHAPE

CAP TEXTURE

CAP DIAMETER

CAP LENGTH

HYMENIUM

SPECIAL PROPERTIES

STALK CHARACTERISTICS

STALK COLOR

STALK SHAPE

STALK TEXTURE

STALK DIAMETER

STALK LENGTH

STALK SURFACE

SPECIAL PROPERTIES

SURROUNDING PLANTS

FAUNA / WILDLIFE

ADDITIONAL NOTES

DATE	WEATHER CONDITIONS

DATE

LOCATION

GPS

WEATHER CONDITIONS

SPECIES / TYPE

SPECIMEN #

TOTAL LENGTH

TYPE OF FOREST

☐ DECIDUOUS	☐ CONIFEROUS
☐ TROPICAL	☐ OTHER

CAP CHARACTERISTICS

CAP COLOR

CAP SHAPE

CAP TEXTURE

CAP DIAMETER

CAP LENGTH

HYMENIUM

SPECIAL PROPERTIES

STALK CHARACTERISTICS

STALK COLOR

STALK SHAPE

STALK TEXTURE

STALK DIAMETER

STALK LENGTH

STALK SURFACE

SPECIAL PROPERTIES

SURROUNDING PLANTS

FAUNA / WILDLIFE

ADDITIONAL NOTES

DATE	
LOCATION	
GPS	

WEATHER CONDITIONS

Temperature: ___ ☀ ⛅ 🌧 ⛈ ❄

Wind: ___ ☐ ☐ ☐ ☐ ☐

SPECIES / TYPE	
SPECIMEN #	
TOTAL LENGTH	

TYPE OF FOREST

☐ DECIDUOUS	☐ CONIFEROUS
☐ TROPICAL	☐ OTHER

CAP CHARACTERISTICS

CAP COLOR	
CAP SHAPE	
CAP TEXTURE	
CAP DIAMETER	
CAP LENGTH	
HYMENIUM	
SPECIAL PROPERTIES	

STALK CHARACTERISTICS

STALK COLOR	
STALK SHAPE	
STALK TEXTURE	
STALK DIAMETER	
STALK LENGTH	
STALK SURFACE	
SPECIAL PROPERTIES	

SURROUNDING PLANTS

FAUNA / WILDLIFE

ADDITIONAL NOTES

DATE		WEATHER CONDITIONS

DATE

LOCATION

GPS

WEATHER CONDITIONS

🌡 ____ ☀ ⛅ 🌧 ⛈ ❄

🎐 ____ ☐ ☐ ☐ ☐ ☐

SPECIES / TYPE

SPECIMEN #

TOTAL LENGTH

TYPE OF FOREST

☐ DECIDUOUS ☐ CONIFEROUS

☐ TROPICAL ☐ OTHER

CAP CHARACTERISTICS

CAP COLOR

CAP SHAPE

CAP TEXTURE

CAP DIAMETER

CAP LENGTH

HYMENIUM

SPECIAL PROPERTIES

STALK CHARACTERISTICS

STALK COLOR

STALK SHAPE

STALK TEXTURE

STALK DIAMETER

STALK LENGTH

STALK SURFACE

SPECIAL PROPERTIES

SURROUNDING PLANTS

FAUNA / WILDLIFE

ADDITIONAL NOTES

DATE

LOCATION

GPS

WEATHER CONDITIONS

☀ ⛅ 🌧 ⛈ ❄

☐	☐	☐	☐	☐

SPECIES / TYPE

SPECIMEN

TOTAL LENGTH

TYPE OF FOREST

☐ DECIDUOUS	☐ CONIFEROUS
☐ TROPICAL	☐ OTHER

CAP CHARACTERISTICS

CAP COLOR

CAP SHAPE

CAP TEXTURE

CAP DIAMETER

CAP LENGTH

HYMENIUM

SPECIAL PROPERTIES

STALK CHARACTERISTICS

STALK COLOR

STALK SHAPE

STALK TEXTURE

STALK DIAMETER

STALK LENGTH

STALK SURFACE

SPECIAL PROPERTIES

SURROUNDING PLANTS

FAUNA / WILDLIFE

ADDITIONAL NOTES

DATE	
LOCATION	
GPS	

WEATHER CONDITIONS

🌡 ___ ☀ ⛅ 🌧 ⛈ ❄

🚩 ___ ☐ ☐ ☐ ☐ ☐

SPECIES / TYPE	
SPECIMEN #	
TOTAL LENGTH	

TYPE OF FOREST

☐ DECIDUOUS	☐ CONIFEROUS
☐ TROPICAL	☐ OTHER

CAP CHARACTERISTICS

CAP COLOR	
CAP SHAPE	
CAP TEXTURE	
CAP DIAMETER	
CAP LENGTH	
HYMENIUM	
SPECIAL PROPERTIES	

STALK CHARACTERISTICS

STALK COLOR	
STALK SHAPE	
STALK TEXTURE	
STALK DIAMETER	
STALK LENGTH	
STALK SURFACE	
SPECIAL PROPERTIES	

SURROUNDING PLANTS

FAUNA / WILDLIFE

ADDITIONAL NOTES

DATE	WEATHER CONDITIONS

| SPECIES / TYPE | TYPE OF FOREST |

DATE

LOCATION

GPS

WEATHER CONDITIONS

🌡 ___ ☀ ⛅ 🌧 ⛈ ❄

🏴 ___ ☐ ☐ ☐ ☐ ☐

SPECIES / TYPE

SPECIMEN #

TOTAL LENGTH

TYPE OF FOREST

☐ DECIDUOUS	☐ CONIFEROUS
☐ TROPICAL	☐ OTHER

CAP CHARACTERISTICS

CAP COLOR

CAP SHAPE

CAP TEXTURE

CAP DIAMETER

CAP LENGTH

HYMENIUM

SPECIAL PROPERTIES

STALK CHARACTERISTICS

STALK COLOR

STALK SHAPE

STALK TEXTURE

STALK DIAMETER

STALK LENGTH

STALK SURFACE

SPECIAL PROPERTIES

SURROUNDING PLANTS

FAUNA / WILDLIFE

ADDITIONAL NOTES

DATE		**WEATHER CONDITIONS**	
LOCATION		☀ ⛅ ☁ 🌧 ⛈ ❄	
GPS		☐ ☐ ☐ ☐ ☐	

SPECIES / TYPE		**TYPE OF FOREST**	
SPECIMEN #		☐ DECIDUOUS	☐ CONIFEROUS
TOTAL LENGTH		☐ TROPICAL	☐ OTHER

CAP CHARACTERISTICS

CAP COLOR
CAP SHAPE
CAP TEXTURE
CAP DIAMETER
CAP LENGTH
HYMENIUM
SPECIAL PROPERTIES

STALK CHARACTERISTICS

STALK COLOR
STALK SHAPE
STALK TEXTURE
STALK DIAMETER
STALK LENGTH
STALK SURFACE
SPECIAL PROPERTIES

SURROUNDING PLANTS

FAUNA / WILDLIFE

ADDITIONAL NOTES

DATE

LOCATION

GPS

WEATHER CONDITIONS

SPECIES / TYPE

SPECIMEN

TOTAL LENGTH

TYPE OF FOREST

| ☐ DECIDUOUS | ☐ CONIFEROUS |
| ☐ TROPICAL | ☐ OTHER |

CAP CHARACTERISTICS

- CAP COLOR
- CAP SHAPE
- CAP TEXTURE
- CAP DIAMETER
- CAP LENGTH
- HYMENIUM
- SPECIAL PROPERTIES

STALK CHARACTERISTICS

- STALK COLOR
- STALK SHAPE
- STALK TEXTURE
- STALK DIAMETER
- STALK LENGTH
- STALK SURFACE
- SPECIAL PROPERTIES

SURROUNDING PLANTS

FAUNA / WILDLIFE

ADDITIONAL NOTES

DATE	
LOCATION	
GPS	

WEATHER CONDITIONS

🌡 ____ ☀ ⛅ 🌧 ⛈ ❄

🏳 ____ ☐ ☐ ☐ ☐ ☐

SPECIES / TYPE	
SPECIMEN #	
TOTAL LENGTH	

TYPE OF FOREST

☐ DECIDUOUS	☐ CONIFEROUS
☐ TROPICAL	☐ OTHER

CAP CHARACTERISTICS

- CAP COLOR
- CAP SHAPE
- CAP TEXTURE
- CAP DIAMETER
- CAP LENGTH
- HYMENIUM
- SPECIAL PROPERTIES

STALK CHARACTERISTICS

- STALK COLOR
- STALK SHAPE
- STALK TEXTURE
- STALK DIAMETER
- STALK LENGTH
- STALK SURFACE
- SPECIAL PROPERTIES

SURROUNDING PLANTS

FAUNA / WILDLIFE

ADDITIONAL NOTES

DATE

LOCATION

GPS

WEATHER CONDITIONS

SPECIES / TYPE

SPECIMEN

TOTAL LENGTH

TYPE OF FOREST

| ☐ DECIDUOUS | ☐ CONIFEROUS |
| ☐ TROPICAL | ☐ OTHER |

CAP CHARACTERISTICS

CAP COLOR

CAP SHAPE

CAP TEXTURE

CAP DIAMETER

CAP LENGTH

HYMENIUM

SPECIAL PROPERTIES

STALK CHARACTERISTICS

STALK COLOR

STALK SHAPE

STALK TEXTURE

STALK DIAMETER

STALK LENGTH

STALK SURFACE

SPECIAL PROPERTIES

SURROUNDING PLANTS

FAUNA / WILDLIFE

ADDITIONAL NOTES

📅 DATE	**WEATHER CONDITIONS**					
📍 LOCATION	🌡️ ___	☀️	⛅	🌧️	⛈️	❄️
🧭 GPS	🎏 ___	☐	☐	☐	☐	☐

🔍 SPECIES / TYPE	**TYPE OF FOREST**	
🗄️ SPECIMEN #	☐ DECIDUOUS	☐ CONIFEROUS
🍄 TOTAL LENGTH	☐ TROPICAL	☐ OTHER

CAP CHARACTERISTICS	**STALK CHARACTERISTICS**
🍄 CAP COLOR	🍄 STALK COLOR
🍄 CAP SHAPE	🍄 STALK SHAPE
🍄 CAP TEXTURE	🍄 STALK TEXTURE
🍄 CAP DIAMETER	🍄 STALK DIAMETER
🍄 CAP LENGTH	🍄 STALK LENGTH
🍄 HYMENIUM	🍄 STALK SURFACE
🍄 SPECIAL PROPERTIES	🍄 SPECIAL PROPERTIES

SURROUNDING PLANTS	**FAUNA / WILDLIFE**

ADDITIONAL NOTES

DATE	WEATHER CONDITIONS

DATE

LOCATION

GPS

WEATHER CONDITIONS

☐ ☐ ☐ ☐ ☐

SPECIES / TYPE

SPECIMEN #

TOTAL LENGTH

TYPE OF FOREST

☐ DECIDUOUS	☐ CONIFEROUS
☐ TROPICAL	☐ OTHER

CAP CHARACTERISTICS

CAP COLOR

CAP SHAPE

CAP TEXTURE

CAP DIAMETER

CAP LENGTH

HYMENIUM

SPECIAL PROPERTIES

STALK CHARACTERISTICS

STALK COLOR

STALK SHAPE

STALK TEXTURE

STALK DIAMETER

STALK LENGTH

STALK SURFACE

SPECIAL PROPERTIES

SURROUNDING PLANTS

FAUNA / WILDLIFE

ADDITIONAL NOTES

DATE

LOCATION

GPS

WEATHER CONDITIONS

☼ ⛅ 🌧 ⛈ ❄

☐ ☐ ☐ ☐ ☐

SPECIES / TYPE

SPECIMEN

TOTAL LENGTH

TYPE OF FOREST

| ☐ DECIDUOUS | ☐ CONIFEROUS |
| ☐ TROPICAL | ☐ OTHER |

CAP CHARACTERISTICS

CAP COLOR

CAP SHAPE

CAP TEXTURE

CAP DIAMETER

CAP LENGTH

HYMENIUM

SPECIAL PROPERTIES

STALK CHARACTERISTICS

STALK COLOR

STALK SHAPE

STALK TEXTURE

STALK DIAMETER

STALK LENGTH

STALK SURFACE

SPECIAL PROPERTIES

SURROUNDING PLANTS

FAUNA / WILDLIFE

ADDITIONAL NOTES

DATE

LOCATION

GPS

WEATHER CONDITIONS

SPECIES / TYPE

SPECIMEN

TOTAL LENGTH

TYPE OF FOREST

☐ DECIDUOUS	☐ CONIFEROUS
☐ TROPICAL	☐ OTHER

CAP CHARACTERISTICS

CAP COLOR

CAP SHAPE

CAP TEXTURE

CAP DIAMETER

CAP LENGTH

HYMENIUM

SPECIAL PROPERTIES

STALK CHARACTERISTICS

STALK COLOR

STALK SHAPE

STALK TEXTURE

STALK DIAMETER

STALK LENGTH

STALK SURFACE

SPECIAL PROPERTIES

SURROUNDING PLANTS

FAUNA / WILDLIFE

ADDITIONAL NOTES

DATE	WEATHER CONDITIONS

DATE

LOCATION

GPS

WEATHER CONDITIONS

☀ ⛅ ☁ 🌧 ⛈ ❄

☐ ☐ ☐ ☐ ☐

SPECIES / TYPE

SPECIMEN #

TOTAL LENGTH

TYPE OF FOREST

☐ DECIDUOUS ☐ CONIFEROUS

☐ TROPICAL ☐ OTHER

CAP CHARACTERISTICS

CAP COLOR

CAP SHAPE

CAP TEXTURE

CAP DIAMETER

CAP LENGTH

HYMENIUM

SPECIAL PROPERTIES

STALK CHARACTERISTICS

STALK COLOR

STALK SHAPE

STALK TEXTURE

STALK DIAMETER

STALK LENGTH

STALK SURFACE

SPECIAL PROPERTIES

SURROUNDING PLANTS

FAUNA / WILDLIFE

ADDITIONAL NOTES

DATE

LOCATION

GPS

WEATHER CONDITIONS

SPECIES / TYPE

SPECIMEN

TOTAL LENGTH

TYPE OF FOREST

DECIDUOUS	CONIFEROUS
TROPICAL	OTHER

CAP CHARACTERISTICS

CAP COLOR

CAP SHAPE

CAP TEXTURE

CAP DIAMETER

CAP LENGTH

HYMENIUM

SPECIAL PROPERTIES

STALK CHARACTERISTICS

STALK COLOR

STALK SHAPE

STALK TEXTURE

STALK DIAMETER

STALK LENGTH

STALK SURFACE

SPECIAL PROPERTIES

SURROUNDING PLANTS

FAUNA / WILDLIFE

ADDITIONAL NOTES

| DATE |
| LOCATION |
| GPS |

WEATHER CONDITIONS

🌡 ___ ☀ ⛅ 🌧 ⛈ ❄

🚩 ___ ☐ ☐ ☐ ☐ ☐

| SPECIES / TYPE |
| SPECIMEN # |
| TOTAL LENGTH |

TYPE OF FOREST

| ☐ DECIDUOUS | ☐ CONIFEROUS |
| ☐ TROPICAL | ☐ OTHER |

CAP CHARACTERISTICS

| CAP COLOR |
| CAP SHAPE |
| CAP TEXTURE |
| CAP DIAMETER |
| CAP LENGTH |
| HYMENIUM |
| SPECIAL PROPERTIES |

STALK CHARACTERISTICS

| STALK COLOR |
| STALK SHAPE |
| STALK TEXTURE |
| STALK DIAMETER |
| STALK LENGTH |
| STALK SURFACE |
| SPECIAL PROPERTIES |

SURROUNDING PLANTS

FAUNA / WILDLIFE

ADDITIONAL NOTES

DATE

LOCATION

GPS

WEATHER CONDITIONS

SPECIES / TYPE

SPECIMEN

TOTAL LENGTH

TYPE OF FOREST

| ☐ DECIDUOUS | ☐ CONIFEROUS |
| ☐ TROPICAL | ☐ OTHER |

CAP CHARACTERISTICS

CAP COLOR

CAP SHAPE

CAP TEXTURE

CAP DIAMETER

CAP LENGTH

HYMENIUM

SPECIAL PROPERTIES

STALK CHARACTERISTICS

STALK COLOR

STALK SHAPE

STALK TEXTURE

STALK DIAMETER

STALK LENGTH

STALK SURFACE

SPECIAL PROPERTIES

SURROUNDING PLANTS

FAUNA / WILDLIFE

ADDITIONAL NOTES

DATE	WEATHER CONDITIONS

DATE

LOCATION

GPS

WEATHER CONDITIONS

☀ ⛅ 🌧 ⛈ ❄

☐ ☐ ☐ ☐ ☐

SPECIES / TYPE

SPECIMEN #

TOTAL LENGTH

TYPE OF FOREST

☐ DECIDUOUS	☐ CONIFEROUS
☐ TROPICAL	☐ OTHER

CAP CHARACTERISTICS

CAP COLOR

CAP SHAPE

CAP TEXTURE

CAP DIAMETER

CAP LENGTH

HYMENIUM

SPECIAL PROPERTIES

STALK CHARACTERISTICS

STALK COLOR

STALK SHAPE

STALK TEXTURE

STALK DIAMETER

STALK LENGTH

STALK SURFACE

SPECIAL PROPERTIES

SURROUNDING PLANTS

FAUNA / WILDLIFE

ADDITIONAL NOTES

DATE

LOCATION

GPS

WEATHER CONDITIONS

SPECIES / TYPE

SPECIMEN

TOTAL LENGTH

TYPE OF FOREST

	DECIDUOUS		CONIFEROUS
	TROPICAL		OTHER

CAP CHARACTERISTICS

CAP COLOR

CAP SHAPE

CAP TEXTURE

CAP DIAMETER

CAP LENGTH

HYMENIUM

SPECIAL PROPERTIES

STALK CHARACTERISTICS

STALK COLOR

STALK SHAPE

STALK TEXTURE

STALK DIAMETER

STALK LENGTH

STALK SURFACE

SPECIAL PROPERTIES

SURROUNDING PLANTS

FAUNA / WILDLIFE

ADDITIONAL NOTES

DATE

LOCATION

GPS

WEATHER CONDITIONS

SPECIES / TYPE

SPECIMEN

TOTAL LENGTH

TYPE OF FOREST

☐ DECIDUOUS	☐ CONIFEROUS
☐ TROPICAL	☐ OTHER

CAP CHARACTERISTICS

CAP COLOR

CAP SHAPE

CAP TEXTURE

CAP DIAMETER

CAP LENGTH

HYMENIUM

SPECIAL PROPERTIES

STALK CHARACTERISTICS

STALK COLOR

STALK SHAPE

STALK TEXTURE

STALK DIAMETER

STALK LENGTH

STALK SURFACE

SPECIAL PROPERTIES

SURROUNDING PLANTS

FAUNA / WILDLIFE

ADDITIONAL NOTES

DATE

LOCATION

GPS

WEATHER CONDITIONS

SPECIES / TYPE

SPECIMEN

TOTAL LENGTH

TYPE OF FOREST

DECIDUOUS	CONIFEROUS
TROPICAL	OTHER

CAP CHARACTERISTICS

CAP COLOR

CAP SHAPE

CAP TEXTURE

CAP DIAMETER

CAP LENGTH

HYMENIUM

SPECIAL PROPERTIES

STALK CHARACTERISTICS

STALK COLOR

STALK SHAPE

STALK TEXTURE

STALK DIAMETER

STALK LENGTH

STALK SURFACE

SPECIAL PROPERTIES

SURROUNDING PLANTS

FAUNA / WILDLIFE

ADDITIONAL NOTES

DATE

LOCATION

GPS

WEATHER CONDITIONS

SPECIES / TYPE

SPECIMEN

TOTAL LENGTH

TYPE OF FOREST

| ☐ DECIDUOUS | ☐ CONIFEROUS |
| ☐ TROPICAL | ☐ OTHER |

CAP CHARACTERISTICS

CAP COLOR	
CAP SHAPE	
CAP TEXTURE	
CAP DIAMETER	
CAP LENGTH	
HYMENIUM	
SPECIAL PROPERTIES	

STALK CHARACTERISTICS

STALK COLOR	
STALK SHAPE	
STALK TEXTURE	
STALK DIAMETER	
STALK LENGTH	
STALK SURFACE	
SPECIAL PROPERTIES	

SURROUNDING PLANTS

FAUNA / WILDLIFE

ADDITIONAL NOTES

DATE

LOCATION

GPS

WEATHER CONDITIONS

SPECIES / TYPE

SPECIMEN

TOTAL LENGTH

TYPE OF FOREST

☐ DECIDUOUS		☐ CONIFEROUS	
☐ TROPICAL		☐ OTHER	

CAP CHARACTERISTICS

CAP COLOR

CAP SHAPE

CAP TEXTURE

CAP DIAMETER

CAP LENGTH

HYMENIUM

SPECIAL PROPERTIES

STALK CHARACTERISTICS

STALK COLOR

STALK SHAPE

STALK TEXTURE

STALK DIAMETER

STALK LENGTH

STALK SURFACE

SPECIAL PROPERTIES

SURROUNDING PLANTS

FAUNA / WILDLIFE

ADDITIONAL NOTES

DATE

LOCATION

GPS

WEATHER CONDITIONS

☐ ☐ ☐ ☐ ☐

SPECIES / TYPE

SPECIMEN

TOTAL LENGTH

TYPE OF FOREST

☐ DECIDUOUS	☐ CONIFEROUS
☐ TROPICAL	☐ OTHER

CAP CHARACTERISTICS

CAP COLOR

CAP SHAPE

CAP TEXTURE

CAP DIAMETER

CAP LENGTH

HYMENIUM

SPECIAL PROPERTIES

STALK CHARACTERISTICS

STALK COLOR

STALK SHAPE

STALK TEXTURE

STALK DIAMETER

STALK LENGTH

STALK SURFACE

SPECIAL PROPERTIES

SURROUNDING PLANTS

FAUNA / WILDLIFE

ADDITIONAL NOTES

DATE

LOCATION

GPS

WEATHER CONDITIONS

SPECIES / TYPE

SPECIMEN

TOTAL LENGTH

TYPE OF FOREST

☐ DECIDUOUS	☐ CONIFEROUS
☐ TROPICAL	☐ OTHER

CAP CHARACTERISTICS

CAP COLOR

CAP SHAPE

CAP TEXTURE

CAP DIAMETER

CAP LENGTH

HYMENIUM

SPECIAL PROPERTIES

STALK CHARACTERISTICS

STALK COLOR

STALK SHAPE

STALK TEXTURE

STALK DIAMETER

STALK LENGTH

STALK SURFACE

SPECIAL PROPERTIES

SURROUNDING PLANTS

FAUNA / WILDLIFE

ADDITIONAL NOTES

📅 DATE		**WEATHER CONDITIONS**					
📍 LOCATION		🌡️ ____	☀️	⛅	🌧️	⛈️	❄️
🧭 GPS		🚩 ____	☐	☐	☐	☐	☐

🔍 SPECIES / TYPE	**TYPE OF FOREST**	
🗄️ SPECIMEN #	☐ DECIDUOUS	☐ CONIFEROUS
🍄 TOTAL LENGTH	☐ TROPICAL	☐ OTHER

CAP CHARACTERISTICS	**STALK CHARACTERISTICS**
🍄 CAP COLOR	🍄 STALK COLOR
🍄 CAP SHAPE	🍄 STALK SHAPE
🔬 CAP TEXTURE	🔬 STALK TEXTURE
📏 CAP DIAMETER	📏 STALK DIAMETER
🍄 CAP LENGTH	🍄 STALK LENGTH
🔘 HYMENIUM	🍄 STALK SURFACE
🍄 SPECIAL PROPERTIES	🍄 SPECIAL PROPERTIES

SURROUNDING PLANTS	**FAUNA / WILDLIFE**

ADDITIONAL NOTES

DATE

LOCATION

GPS

WEATHER CONDITIONS

🌡 ____ ☀ ⛅ 🌧 ⛈ ❄

🚩 ____ ☐ ☐ ☐ ☐ ☐

SPECIES / TYPE

SPECIMEN

TOTAL LENGTH

TYPE OF FOREST

☐ DECIDUOUS	☐ CONIFEROUS
☐ TROPICAL	☐ OTHER

CAP CHARACTERISTICS

CAP COLOR

CAP SHAPE

CAP TEXTURE

CAP DIAMETER

CAP LENGTH

HYMENIUM

SPECIAL PROPERTIES

STALK CHARACTERISTICS

STALK COLOR

STALK SHAPE

STALK TEXTURE

STALK DIAMETER

STALK LENGTH

STALK SURFACE

SPECIAL PROPERTIES

SURROUNDING PLANTS

FAUNA / WILDLIFE

ADDITIONAL NOTES

📅 **DATE**	**WEATHER CONDITIONS**
📍 **LOCATION**	🌡️ ___ ☀️ ⛅ 🌧️ ⛈️ ❄️
🧭 **GPS**	🚩 ___ ☐ ☐ ☐ ☐ ☐

🔍 **SPECIES / TYPE**	**TYPE OF FOREST**	
📦 **SPECIMEN #**	☐ DECIDUOUS	☐ CONIFEROUS
🍄 **TOTAL LENGTH**	☐ TROPICAL	☐ OTHER

CAP CHARACTERISTICS	**STALK CHARACTERISTICS**
🍄 CAP COLOR	🍄 STALK COLOR
🍄 CAP SHAPE	🍄 STALK SHAPE
🔮 CAP TEXTURE	🔮 STALK TEXTURE
◯ CAP DIAMETER	◯ STALK DIAMETER
🍄 CAP LENGTH	🍄 STALK LENGTH
🎯 HYMENIUM	🍄 STALK SURFACE
🍄 SPECIAL PROPERTIES	🍄 SPECIAL PROPERTIES

SURROUNDING PLANTS	**FAUNA / WILDLIFE**

ADDITIONAL NOTES

DATE	WEATHER CONDITIONS

DATE

LOCATION

GPS

WEATHER CONDITIONS

SPECIES / TYPE	TYPE OF FOREST

SPECIES / TYPE

SPECIMEN

TOTAL LENGTH

TYPE OF FOREST

☐ DECIDUOUS	☐ CONIFEROUS
☐ TROPICAL	☐ OTHER

CAP CHARACTERISTICS

CAP COLOR

CAP SHAPE

CAP TEXTURE

CAP DIAMETER

CAP LENGTH

HYMENIUM

SPECIAL PROPERTIES

STALK CHARACTERISTICS

STALK COLOR

STALK SHAPE

STALK TEXTURE

STALK DIAMETER

STALK LENGTH

STALK SURFACE

SPECIAL PROPERTIES

SURROUNDING PLANTS

FAUNA / WILDLIFE

ADDITIONAL NOTES

DATE

LOCATION

GPS

WEATHER CONDITIONS

🌡 —— ☀ ⛅ 🌧 ⛈ ❄

🏳 —— ☐ ☐ ☐ ☐ ☐

SPECIES / TYPE

SPECIMEN

TOTAL LENGTH

TYPE OF FOREST

☐ DECIDUOUS	☐ CONIFEROUS
☐ TROPICAL	☐ OTHER

CAP CHARACTERISTICS

CAP COLOR

CAP SHAPE

CAP TEXTURE

CAP DIAMETER

CAP LENGTH

HYMENIUM

SPECIAL PROPERTIES

STALK CHARACTERISTICS

STALK COLOR

STALK SHAPE

STALK TEXTURE

STALK DIAMETER

STALK LENGTH

STALK SURFACE

SPECIAL PROPERTIES

SURROUNDING PLANTS

FAUNA / WILDLIFE

ADDITIONAL NOTES

Made in the USA
Coppell, TX
20 June 2022

79052142R00070